THE MAKING OF LATE ANTIQUITY

CARL NEWELL JACKSON LECTURES

THE MAKING
OF
LATE ANTIQUITY

PETER BROWN

Harvard University Press
Cambridge, Massachusetts
and London, England

First Harvard University Press paperback edition, 1993

Library of Congress Cataloging in Publication Data
Brown, Peter Robert Lamont.
The making of late antiquity.

(The Carl Newell Jackson lectures; 1976)
Includes index.
1. Rome—History—Empire, 284–476—Addresses,
essays, lectures. 2. Church history—Primitive and
early Church, ca.30–600—Addresses, essays, lectures.
I. Title. II. Series.
DG312.B76   937'.06   78-6844
ISBN 0-674-54320-3 (cloth)
ISBN 0-674-54321-1 (paper)

For Sabine

In memory of a common friend

Gervase Mathew, O.P.

. . . Πιστὸν ὁδηγόν . . .

Παρὰ τοῦ κυρίου ἀιτησώμεθα

—*Liturgy of St. John Chrysostom*

ACKNOWLEDGMENTS

This book contains a slightly expanded and revised version of the four Carl Newell Jackson Lectures that I had the honor to deliver at Harvard University in April 1976. My gratitude to the eminent founder of these lectures can only be incompletely expressed in these few pages.

The Department of Classics and its chairman, Glen Bowersock—*comes* and, for much of the time, a discreetly courteous *tribunus voluptatum*—together with so many senior and junior members of Harvard University, made a solemn and potentially taxing experience into an occasion to learn more every day in an atmosphere of unmodified delight.

The work for these lectures was begun in the University of California, at Berkeley, and was continued in the History Department of Royal Holloway College, at the University of London. I would be happy if the reader should perceive, as I would wish him to, that some of the warmth and intellectual stimulation of those two environments has lingered in these pages. For it is there, as also among those many figures at Harvard, whom I had long admired and then found to be friends as well as colleagues and sure-footed guides, that I have been reminded of the wise words put into the mouth of the Apostle in the Pseudo-Clementine *Recognitiones:*

> *ex mundo tempus, et ex hoc hominum multitudo*
> *ex multitudine electio amicorum, ex quorum*
> *unanimitate pacificum construitur dei regnum.*

Pseudo-Clement, *Recognitiones* I, 24, 3

Last, but not least, Rita Townsend and Susan Barlow, in the midst of manifold duties, have unfailingly given me the reassurance of impeccable and intelligent typing.

P.B.

CONTENTS

THE MAKING OF LATE ANTIQUITY

1

A DEBATE
ON THE HOLY

I wish that I had been one of the Seven Sleepers of Ephesus. These Christian brothers had been walled up in a cave in the middle of the third century, during the pagan persecution of the Emperor Decius (249–251). They were awakened in the early fifth century, in the reign of Decius' direct successor, the Emperor Theodosius II (408–450), in order to enlighten that most Christian monarch on a point concerning the resurrection of the dead. Imagine their surprise when, on entering the city, they saw the Cross placed above the main gate, heard men freely swearing by the name of Christ, saw a great church and the Christian clergy busied with repairing the walls of the city, and found that the solid silver coins of a pagan emperor caused amazement in the marketplace.[1]

This book is an attempt to enter into their surprise. Hence the title—*The Making of Late Antiquity*. I wish to trace in the late second, third, and early fourth centuries the emergence of features that were far from clearly discernible at the time when our Christian brothers entered the cave and which finally came together to form the definitively Late Antique style of religious, cultural, and social life that emerged in the late fourth and early fifth centuries.

Although all of two centuries elapsed between the age of the Antonines and the death of Constantine, the third century A.D. must lie at the center of any account of the making of Late Antiquity. The changes associated with that century have been held to mark no less than the "watershed between the Ancient World and the European Middle Ages."[2] Such a description of the third century is likely to remain the subject of prolonged debate.[3] It is important to be clear what is at stake in such a debate. It is not whether, at some point between Marcus Aurelius and Constantine—two emperors who have been conventionally considered to sum up in their own persons and in the quality of their reigns the opposite poles of a pagan, classical world and the Christian Late Roman Empire—a watershed was passed. The real problem is what it is like for a great traditional society to pass over a watershed.

We must look closely at the overall features of the environment in which the changes took place. Only in this way can we avoid from the outset those anachronisms that have encouraged modern scholars to invest the religious and social changes associated with the making of Late Antiquity with a false air of melodrama. We have to begin with a sense of the limitations imposed on life in the ancient Mediterranean. Factors we would regard as natural in a "crisis"— *malaise* caused by urbanization, public disasters, the intrusion of alien religious ideas, and a consequent heightening of religious hopes and fears—may not have bulked as large in the minds of the men of the late second and third centuries as we suppose.

Thus, many modern accounts of the religious evolution of the Roman world place great emphasis on the *malaise* of life in great cities in Hellenistic and Roman times. Yet the loneliness of the great city and the rapid deculturation of immigrants from traditionalist areas are modern ills: they should not be overworked as explanatory devices for the society we are studying. We can be far from certain that "such loneliness must have been felt by millions—the urbanized tribesman, the peasant come to town in search of work."[4] When a distinguished scholar ascribes changes in religious sensibility associated with the proliferation of the Hermetic literature in the second century A.D. to the pressure of urban conditions and asserts that "la civilisation gréco-romaine est déjà une civilisation de grandes villes. Dans ces grandes villes la majorité des habitants vivent comme aujourd'hui," we can only disagree.[5]

The towns of the Mediterranean were small towns.[6] For all their isolation from the way of life of the villagers, they were fragile excrescences in a spreading countryside. As in medieval Italy, "Everywhere the country thrust its tendrils into the town."[7] Not every tendril was innocent: wild animals drifted into the towns of North Africa, making their lairs in the basements and eating the citizens.[8] Like the country folk, the townsmen lived with their eyes on the sky. Throughout this period, the weather was a more pertinacious persecutor of religious dissent than was any emperor: the *caelites*, the inhabitants of the sky, plural or singular, spoke most forcibly in the sudden hailstorm and in the brazen drought and showed their pleasure most convincingly in the waving wheatfields.[9] As the pagan Emperor Maximin Daia wrote in 311 to the city of Tyre: "Let them cast their eyes on the wide plains, where already the crops are ripe with waving ears of corn, and the meadows, thanks to the abundance of rain, are bright with flowering plants, and the weather we enjoy is temperate and very mild."[10] *Pacis haec et annonae otia. Ab imperio et a caelo bene est.*[11]

In such towns we move among small human groups. The "face-to-face" community is the unit of Late Antique religious history. Rome and the great "capital" cities of the later Empire remained exceptional. Even in the greatest cities, we know far less than we might about the stability of the population and its tendency to coagulate into *quartiers* that were as stable and as intimate as any villages. Wherever we have the evidence, we can sense the outlines of the basic "cells" of urban life: crowded streets where everyone knew each other;[12] small professional associations that collaborated vigorously in maintaining traditional social controls;[13] a world with very little privacy, where the non-participant was only too readily recognized.[14] In Rome, Galen longed for the social controls of the average small town where "we all know each other, know who was whose son, what education each of us had received, how much property each owned, and how each one of us behaved."[15] The stones of every town in Asia Minor bear him out. Those egregious catalogues of normative values in Greek honorific inscriptions from the first to the sixth century A.D. betray the unremitting discipline imposed on the actors of the small and unbearably well lit stage of an ancient city.[16] If anything, claustrophobia and the tensions of living in a face-to-face society, not loneliness or rootlessness, are the leitmotifs of the specifically Late Antique form of being unhappy.

It is also important to maintain a sense of perspective about the areas of Mediterranean life on which the known political vicissitues of the third century impinged. There is a danger that we may draw the nets of explanation too tightly around the average inhabitant of the Roman world. A period of military defeat and of undeniable insecurity among the governing classes of the Roman Empire may not have had repercussions in Roman society at large sufficiently drastic to produce, by way of immediate reaction, the religious changes we ascribe to this period. It is for this reason that I have long been dissatisfied with the idea of a general "crisis" of the third century as a *passe-partout* explanation for the emergence of the distinctive features of Late Antique religion. I cannot believe that the phenomena I will have to describe can be explained, as E. R. Dodds once thought to explain an aspect of them, as the revulsion of men "from a world so impoverished intellectually, so insecure materially, so filled with fear and hatred as the world of the third century."[17] This is not only because I am not fully convinced that the third-century world was like that; it is because I have learned from Professor Dodds more than from any other living scholar that men are not so simple, and so do not react to their circumstances in so simple a manner.

Before we talk of anxiety and disillusionment as both pervasive and distinguishing features of the third century, we have to be very certain that the awareness of life's possibilities was any more bright in the periods that provided the men of the third century with the means of assessing their circumstances. Disillusionment assumes illusion, and ancient men kept themselves studiously free of illusions about what life could offer to them. A man making his will was expected to envisage violent death at the hands of "the enemy, of brigands, or through the cruelty or hatred of some powerful man"[18]—and this in the "Golden Age" of the Antonines! When it came to the public life of the Empire, a man like Seneca could hardly have set his sights much lower: "Ultimately Seneca was unable to explain in clear words why he cared for political life, and he had no constructive thought about it. His best, most profound, words were about private virtues and intimate feelings."[19] Therefore, if, for certain classes at certain moments in the third century "the epoch turned black,"[20] this may mean no more than that it turned a slightly deeper shade of the ever expected grey.

The invocation of pervasive moods and of public misfortunes overlooks the bitter precision of life's small heart-

breaks. A series of questions posed to an oracle in Oxyrhynchus has been made famous by Rostovtzeff as evidence for
the deepening insecurity of the time:

> Shall I be sold up?
> Am I to become a beggar?
> Shall I take to flight?

But the troubles of an Egyptian townsman did not end there:

> Shall I obtain benefit from my friend?
> Shall I be reconciled with my wife?
> Shall I get a divorce?
> Have I been bewitched?[21]

These, the *grandeur et misère* of life in a small community,
are the humus from which profound religious and cultural
changes spring. The religious historian, just because he
is a religious historian, must be "concrete and fastidious."
He needs a sense of life lived twenty-four hours in the day.
The Roman Empire into which he must try to peer is like
that remembered by Marcus Aurelius:

> Think, by way of illustration on the times of Vespasian, and
> thou shalt see all these things: mankind marrying, rearing
> children, sickening, dying, warring, making holiday, traffick-
> ing, tilling, flattering others, vaunting themselves, scheming,
> praying for the death of others, murmuring at their own lot,
> hoarding, covetting a consulate, covetting a kingdom.[22]

Compared with the flesh and blood that the religious historian demands, much of the conventional political and
administrative history of the Later Roman Empire is an
airy wraith.

Therefore, if the religious changes of the third century
cannot be reduced to so many "reactions" to public calamity,
these changes must be sought out in more intimate areas and
over a wider time span—in the slow moving religious life
of the city, the *quartier*, and the family. In this case, it becomes

essential to develop an accurate sense of how a firmly rooted traditional society reacts to religious change. Some scholars emphasize the impact of alien ideas and of alien cults as primary causes of the end of classical pagan civilization and tend to present the religious changes of the third century as the final breaking through of intrusive elements that had built up in the Roman world over previous centuries. In so doing, they assume a rigidity and a vulnerability in later classical paganism that exists more in their own, idealized image of such a paganism than in the realities of the second century A.D.[23] The Roman world of the age of the Antonines was both more flexible and had been more effectively "immunized" to the emergence of new elements than appears at first sight.

The Mediterranean basin, as Plutarch saw it, was already "a well-mixed bowl of myths."[24] The historian of Late Antiquity who wishes to turn philologist and to live among texts will soon find that there is nothing new under the sun. This is a salutary experience. For it firmly removes the temptation to interpret the religious evolution of Late Antiquity in terms of the dramatic "diffusion" of novel ideas from specific *loci*; least of all can it leave room for the view that sees the rise of a Late Antique civilization as due to the drifting of so many alien thistle seeds into the tidy garden of classical Greco-Roman culture. The inhabitants of the Mediterranean towns had long possessed a finely articulated and embracing *koiné* of religious and social experience. The words and habits by which new options might be cogently expressed already existed in readily communicable form. The religious history of the third and fourth centuries would have its shocks; but I would suggest that these shocks are better understood as so many cases of spontaneous combustion arising from friction within a system of widely shared ideas and not as the irruption from the outside of so many

"Jewish," "oriental," "lower class," or "superstitious" elements.[25]

It follows from this that the changes that come about in Late Antiquity can best be seen as a redistribution and a reorchestration of components that had already existed for centuries in the Mediterranean world. From the point of view of religious language, Late Antiquity is always later than we think. In a characteristically warm image, the late Henri-Irenée Marrou has likened the impromptu performances of the master rhetoricians of the late classical age to the virtuoso techniques of a Hot Jazz trumpeter; they could bring out themes deeply embedded in their own memory and held at readiness for themselves and their hearers by centuries of tradition and could weave such themes into new combinations. These new combinations often had a topical relevance all the more cogent for being expressed in ancient, easily intelligible terms.[26] In a similar manner, we find in Late Antiquity ancient themes woven into startling patterns. We begin with a world where so many of the religious and philosophical constituents of Late Antiquity are already present. Paul, Philo, the Gnostics, not to mention those disturbing *revenants* of an earlier age of Greek thought, Pythagoras and Empedocles, are already in the air;[27] but we have to wait many generations before these well-known themes come together to form the unmistakable late Roman sound.

We are dealing, therefore, with a very old world. In it, changes did not come as disturbing visitations from outside; they happened all the more forcibly for having been pieced together from ancient and familiar materials. In that case, we must be careful to avoid melodramatic insistence on sudden and widespread changes in the climate of religious belief in the Mediterranean world of the second and third centuries. Instead, we have to make the considerable imaginative leap of entering into a world where religion was taken absolutely for granted and belief in the supernatural occasioned far less excitement than we might at first sight suppose. Mediterranean men shared their world with invisible beings, largely more powerful than themselves, to whom they had to relate. They did this with the same sense of unavoidable obligation as they experienced in wide areas of their relations with more visible neighbors. When a sixth-century Christian lady in Egypt made her will, distributing her goods between visible and invisible recipients, it is only we who would call her "pious" or "superstitious" or a "conventional Christian": she was merely doing her duty as a human being.[28] When, centuries earlier, crowds had streamed out at festivals, they were not being "conservative" or "pagan"; they were simply enjoying being human at its best—going out to meet the gods;[29] and their Christian fellows had begun to do the same, trooping to church *studio sollemnitatis et publicae quodammodo remissionis.*[30]

Modern scholars are in varying degrees the heirs of the Romantic movement of northern Europe. They have tended to emphasize the subjective religious experience as the stuff of religious history. The labels they have evolved fit ill on the massive realism of the ancient, Mediterranean, view of religion. Words like "conservative" or "traditionalist," ethically weighted dichotomies between "personal" and "collective," "external" and "internal," "sincere" and "unthinking" are inapplicable to the study of this period. Nor is it possible to make a distinction between the "unthinking" masses and the sophisticated agonizings of a small leisured minority and to concentrate our attention exclusively on the latter. In a world haunted by underemployment, far more people than we might imagine had time to think and to argue; and religion provided them with a universally available and sophisticated language with which to do so.[31]

A study of the religious evolution of Late Antiquity that consists largely in the search for areas of high emotional temperature is misconceived. For if the invisible world was as real as the visible, then it could be taken for granted in the same way—no greater emotional pressure was required to relate to a god than to a neighbor. We must at all costs avoid doing the feeling for Late Antique men. Reserves of credulity, of anxiety, and of pious horror, quite surprising to find in modern Western scholars, have been lavished on their behalf: "High and low, Christian or pagan, the whole age was dominated by supernatural forces."[32] Faced with such certainty on the part of a sober historian as to the flavor of Late Antique life, it is good to be reminded of the sang-froid of a late sixth-century Egyptian couple:

> Aurelius Theodore, a baker, and Aurelia Amaresia, daughter of a merchant, both of Antinopolis, declare: "we were in time past joined to one another in marriage and community of life in fair hopes and with a view to the procreation of legitimate children, thinking to maintain a peaceful and seemly married life with one another for the whole time of our joint lives; but on the contrary we have suffered from a sinister and wicked demon which attacked us unexpectedly from we know not whence, with a view to our being separated from one another." After which they get down to business details, abandoning all reciprocal claims and specifying that either party may make a second marriage.

Late Antique men were neither more nor less *insouciant* and hard-headed than men who share the world with invisible neighbors can be observed to be.[34] I would wish to plead that the modern scholar should, at least, begin his study of them by setting aside holy dread. Many of the religious histories of the Late Antique period have tended to place their main emphasis on emotional and subjective qualities and have spoken of the emergence of Late Antique civilization in terms of a rise of "superstition," of a "failure of nerve," or of a "decline of rationalism." In so doing, they seem to miss the point. Indeed, if judged simply in terms of religious ferment, Late Antiquity is a singularly sober and serious-minded period in European history. There is nothing in it as drastic as the landslide of the Dionysiac movement, nor as sudden as the fusing together of the early Islamic theocracy; and, by the robust standards of later medieval and early modern Europe, there is the merest wan flicker of a pursuit of the millennium.

In this study, I would wish to offer to the classical scholar a different manner of narrating the religious and social changes of the period between Marcus Aurelius and the death of Constantine. It seems to me that the world to which the Seven Sleepers awoke was one in which the *locus* of the supernatural had come to shift significantly. Throughout the whole period, certain expectations of the supernatural remained remarkably constant. In the words of Arthur Darby Nock: "We may assert that one of the notes of much belief in its evolution under the Empire is that it is directed to divine power rather than to divine personalities." [35] What changed in no uncertain manner, however, between the second and the fifth centuries, were men's views as to where exactly this "divine power" was to be found on earth and, consequently, on what terms access to it could be achieved.

In this period, "divine power" came to be defined with increasing clarity as the opposite of all other forms of power. The "*locus* of the supernatural," where this unique power was operative, came to stand for a zone in human life where decisions, obligations, experiences, and information were deemed to come from outside the human community. A highly privileged area of human behavior and of human relations was demarcated. Whatever took place in relation to this *locus* and, more particularly, whatever claims to obedience were made within its territory were thought of as being removed to a quite exceptional degree—ideally, removed totally—from the ambiguity, the criticism, the envy, and the resentment that were observed to attend the impingement on fellow human beings of mere human skill, human force, and human powers of persuasion. The *"locus* of the supernatural,"* thus defined, placed a full stop to the normal unfolding of competitiveness and uncertainty.

In the period between 200 and 400, Mediterranean men came to accept, in increasing numbers and with increasing enthusiasm, the idea that this "divine power" did not only manifest itself directly to the average individual or through perennially established institutions: rather "divine power" was represented on earth by a limited number of exceptional human agents, who had been empowered to bring it to bear among their fellows by reason of a relationship with the supernatural that was personal to them, stable and clearly perceptible to fellow believers.

Hence the importance, in this period, of the rise of the Christian church. The Christian church was the *impresario* of a wider change. Its organization and the careers of its heroes made brutally explicit the consequences of the focusing of "divine power" on human beings. The Christian church produced the Apostles, whose deeds were remembered, and gained in the telling, in the Christian communities, the martyrs of the second and third centuries, the already formidable bishops of the later third century, and finally, the succession of great holy men of ascetic origin who ringed the settled communities of the Eastern Mediterranean, from Saint Anthony onwards.[36] Radically new and abiding institutions grew up around men on whom the divine *dignatio* was held to rest in an irreversible manner, whether these were the Christian communities organized by men of the caliber of Cyprian or the new monastic settlements of

Pachomius. In later centuries, individual Christian holy men impinged on all classes of the east Roman world because they were believed to be tangible links between heaven and earth. Nothing made their role as specifically human agents of the supernatural more plain than the moment when they were shown at their most human—that is, when they died. At that moment, a link in the chain joining heaven and earth was severed. Bishop Serapion of Thmuis wrote to the disciples of Anthony in 356: "Consider now: the very moment when the Great Man of our land, the blessed Anthony who prayed for the whole world, passed from us, the wrath of God is come upon Egypt and all things are overturned and become calamitous."[37]

Let us, therefore, compare the two ages, between which the shift in the *locus* of the supernatural became increasingly apparent. In about 400, the direct descendants of men who, in the age of the Antonines, had placed their hopes in times of illness on the invisible and timeless Asclepius, a kindly figure of their dream world, turned in increasing numbers to visible, mortal human beings to whom God had "transferred" the power of healing.[38] Oracular statements that had once been delivered by the invisible gods through mediums rendered transparent to their voice by trance were now sought from the "holy lips" of men. A man like John of Lycopolis, whom the Emperor Theodosius I consulted on the eve of his last campaign, in 394, was expected to keep his wits about him and to draw his claim to belief from a carefully maintained lifestyle, not from the discontinuous plucking of the fingers of God on his soul.[39]

A society prepared to vest fellow humans with such powers was ever vigilant. Men watched each other closely for those signs of intimacy with the supernatural that would validate their claim. Holiness itself might be quantifiable. Symeon Stylites, we are told, touched his toes 1,244 times in bowing before God from the top of his column. The true horror of this story lies not in the exertions of the saint, but in the layman who stood there counting.[40]

Agents of the supernatural existed and could be seen to exist. Seldom has an age mobilized such skill in representing the faces of those men thought to be in contact with the divine. Late Antique portraiture shows how such men were expected to be remembered: "not elegant . . . but majestic and sedate."[41]

Literary portraiture in the form of biography and auto-biography flourished: the *Acts of the Martyrs*; Eusebius' *Life of Constantine*, a work whose capacity to irritate the modern historian springs precisely from its Late Antique aim: how to present the career of a successful autocrat "as a model of the pious life";[42] Athanasius' *Life of Anthony*; Augustine's *Confessions*; and, last but not least, the long portrait gallery of pagan philosophers whose unnerving features still flustered the good Patriarch Photius as he read through his copy of the *Vita Isidori* by Damascius in the ninth century, always protesting, always reading on. Such works are the product of *milieux* that expected the values of a religion, of a learned tradition, or of a culture to be summed up and made operative among men in outstanding individuals. Hagiography served as a magnifying glass to focus into the burning pinpoint of one man's life the sun of "divine power" that shone, if more diffusely, over the group as a whole: the group of fellow believers, also, was "separate" from society, and ultimately superior to it, by reason of its permanent closeness to the supernatural.

Late Antiquity, in both its pagan and its Christian forms, can almost be seen as a playing in reverse of the *Hippolytus* of Euripides. In few periods of history since the troubled days of the sixth century B.C. had Mediterranean men so recklessly flouted the hard-bitten message of that great tragedy: "To hate the proud reserve that owns few friends."[43] Outright superiorities in individuals and unbridgeable differences between the members of a group and those outside it are accepted and expressed with ever greater clarity. Some men are recognized as being permanently closer to the supernatural than others: their actions and commands are exempted from the ambiguities of normal human society, and the groups that they form cut across the normal tissue of human relations.

The rise to ever greater prominence of human agents of the supernatural in no way exhausts our picture of Late Antique civilization as a whole. The development itself culminated among Late Antique men who managed to combine the assiduous consultation of holy men with impenitent secular traditions.[44] Furthermore, the emphasis on human bearers of "divine power" was held in check by other strands in the religious thought of the age. Seldom have pagans expressed themselves with such pathos on the suprahuman majesty of the universe, or Christians felt so close to the towering presence of the angels, "the first of God's creation." Yet to stress this particular development has the merit of bringing to our explanations of the religious evolution of Late Antiquity some degree of precision as to what, exactly, needs to be explained. Merely to observe, as many scholars have done, that from the second century A.D. onwards men came to behave and to think in a manner different from modern Europeans, and from the manner we would like to believe that Greeks and Romans of more "classical" ages had behaved and thought, advances our understanding of what actually happened in Late Antiquity not an inch. Societies can pass through a "failure of nerve" and can witness a "decline of rationalism" without drawing from the experience the particular consequence of permanently vesting some of their fellows with "divine power." Among many groups, and over long periods of time, belief in the supernatural can be strong, even impulsive. Yet it has often been articulated in such a way as to exclude, or to keep within narrow bounds, the claims of particular human beings to represent the supernatural on earth. What gives Late Antiquity its special flavor is precisely the claims of human beings.

We should not be lulled into taking the development for granted. The situation that brought it about in the course of the third century requires careful analysis. For to vest a fellow human being with powers and claims to loyalty associated with the supernatural, and especially a human being whose claim was not rendered unchallengeable by obvious coercive powers, is a momentous decision for a society made up of small face-to-face groups to make. A mechanism of well-tried devices, limiting what men are expected to do in this life and what can be expected to happen to them at or after physical death, has to slide open. To reduce the sliding open of such locks to a "decline of rationalism" or a "rise of superstition" is to import into the study of ancient religion modern concepts that are too slender. Such vague formulae cannot explain the intricate process by which an ancient society shifted the weights and balances in its ideas and expectancies of what a fellow human being can do and experience, to admit this particular range of possibilities for chosen individuals.

I suspect that all this would have been more clear to one of our Seven Sleepers than it is to us. Let us for a moment breathe with him the air of Late Antiquity. Few ages that have the reputation for being so "other-worldly" were, in fact, more resolutely "upper-worldly." The antithesis of the heavens and the earth, closer to the stars, closer to the heavy matter of our world, *epouranios* and *epigeios*, runs obsessively through the literature of the period.[45] The men we call "agents of the supernatural" were those who had brought down into the dubious and tension-ridden world beneath the moon a clarity and a stability associated with the unchanging heavens. Their position came from having linked the two poles of the Late Antique universe: they had "brought down the binding force of Heaven from the sky."[46] For a Late Antique man, for instance, revelation meant far more than the abandonment of trust in human reason; it meant the joining of two spheres:

> When the Holy One, blessed be he, created the world, he decreed and said, "The heavens are the heavens of the Lord, and the earth he gave to the sons of men" (Ps. 115:16). When he sought to give the Torah, he repealed the first decree and said, Those which are below shall come up, and those which are above shall come down. And I shall begin; as it is written, "And the Lord came down upon Mount Sinai" (Exod. 19:20). And it is also written, "And he said to Moses, Come up to the Lord" (Exod. 24:1).[47]

The religious leader was the man whose heart was on high: *mens caelestis, pectus sublime*.[48] He was joined either directly or by an unconfused chain of intermediaries to the stars. Their tranquil glow and regular movements shone out, Eusebius said, as light streaming from the outer doors of the great palace of Heaven:[49] little wonder that Eusebius would emphasize the manner in which Constantine showed himself on his coins, his eyes raised to that steady and perceptible light.[50] The Milky Way glistened with the souls of those who had held their hearts and eyes high on earth: Vettius Agorius Praetextatus, so his widow believed, was there;[51] so, a century later, was Asclepiodotus of Aphrodisias in Caria.[52] In a Christian grave the time-old paradox would have been driven home with a new vehemence. Although the carver of the inscription might still write *astra fovent animam corpus natura recepit*,[53] a dizzy linking of two poles in the narrow grave could be attested, at the tomb of a saint, by miracles.

Everybody, therefore, was expected to know an accredited agent of the supernatural when they saw one: as the grave Egyptian priest told the young lovers in the *Ethiopica* of Heliodorus: "There is a vulgar science and one which, I might say, crawls on the surface of this earth . . . The other, my son, is truly wise, of which the vulgar form is an illegitimate version masquerading under the same name: this one it is which looks up to heaven, which speaks directly with the gods and shares in the quality of those superior beings."[54]

As this citation shows, Late Antique man also knew the opposite to such an agent. The Late Antique antithesis has to be seen at both ends. One end provided contemporaries with a heady language of admiration. But this admiration did not come easily: the other end gave them a discriminating device of considerable sensitivity and resilience. "Heavenly" use of power assumed its shadow, "earthly" use of power. Just as some human beings could be linked to the clear heavens, so many more were implicated with invisible figures who shared in the ambivalent, shadowy, and tension-ridden quality of the earthly regions: "This wisdom descendeth not from above, but is earthly, sensual, devilish."[55]

The "earthly" region, therefore, was never neutral. Men had to make up their minds about bearers of "heavenly" power in an environment heavy with alternative, if invisible, "earthly" sources of power. They had to be aware of "every unclean spirit that worketh . . . that is under the earth, that is fiery, dark, evil-smelling, given to witchcraft."[56] Exercise of supernatural power from "earthly" sources was only to be expected; but it could be discounted. Even the most impressive feats derived from "earthly" power shared in the deceptive and manipulative qualities of the material world. They could be dismissed as "unreal" in the strict

Late Antique sense, of coming from "powers" that existed but that were not "divine." They were "tricks that delude the senses, and work wonders by magical manipulation, through men who overreach themselves in dealing with the [invisible] powers of this material world."[57]

Thus, far from drawing on unlimited reserves of undifferentiated credulity, a Late Antique man faced the supernatural with a set of cosmic beliefs that had filled his mind with a meticulous and exacting questionnaire as to the alternative sources of any manifestation of the supernatural. This enabled him to assess the possible aims of any human being who used its powers and, by implication, the possible repercussions for himself and his group of a decision to acclaim an individual as the bearer of "heavenly" rather than of "earthly" forms of supernatural power. Thus armed, he was always prepared to give his gift horse a long and critical look in the mouth: "The hour of doom is drawing near, and the moon is cleft in two. Yet when they see a sign the unbelievers turn their backs and say: 'Ingenious magic.'"[58] The frustration so vividly expressed by Muhammad in his *Koran* stands at the end of a long tradition that prevailed in the Mediterranean also. Men believed in both "miracles" and "magic." This was not because their credulity was boundless. It was rather so that they should feel free to exercise a choice as to which wielder of supernatural power they would acclaim as a holy man and which they would dismiss as a sorcerer. The one could receive unalloyed loyalty, the other no more than an enforced and transient respect. It was with this in mind that Augustine was prepared to distinguish two types of "miracle": *quaedam enim sunt, quae solam faciunt admirationem, quaedam vero magnam etiam gratiam benevolentiamque conciliant.*[59]

Just because such language was used so lavishly in controversy in Late Antiquity, we should not dismiss it as

merely a theological or a polemical formula. Nor, because
it was applied most explicitly and pervasively to the figure
of the sorcerer, should it be isolated. The sorcerer was
merely a paradigm of supernatural power misapplied in
society; and the criteria used to judge the source and exercise
of such power involved issues that were far from being
purely theological. For what was condensed in such language
was a muffled debate on the exercise of different forms of
power in small groups.

Hence the emphasis placed throughout this period on
the demonic. This was not because the demons were merely
the declared enemies of the human race. Rather, Late
Antique thought stressed their ambiguous and anomalous
status. To Plutarch, writing at the beginning of our period,
it was a benign ambiguity: the demons were an "elegant
solution" for the incongruities that arose from the joining
of heaven and earth.[60] In later centuries their role changed.
From intermediate beings, they became an active source of
falsehood and illusion in the human race.[61] They gave
dramatic intensity to doubts about how heaven and earth
could be joined and made such doubts a permanent ingredient
in the Late Antique universe. The demons were an order of
far from perfect, one might even say "anomalous," beings.[62]
Their presence in the "earthly" regions introduced a
constant element of indeterminacy and confusion into the
clear structure that linked rightful agents of the supernatural
to their heavenly source. A few men were linked directly to
the higher, stable regions of the universe; most men,
however, partook of the incomplete, ambiguous quality of
the demonic. Thus, with the demons, Late Antique men
found themselves flanked by an invisible society that shared
with them all the incongruities and the tensions of their own,
visible world. The "earthly" power of the demons, on
which the sorcerer drew, was a faithful replication of all

that was sensed as most abrasively egotistic, as most domineering in the social world in which he operated. Thus if any human being were to gain acceptance by any group in Late Antiquity as wielding power based on a peculiar relationship with the supernatural, he would have to make his way in an atmosphere heavy with tacit resentments at power exercised in a manner that threatened merely to replicate, to the disadvantage of his fellows, patterns of domination and dependence current in society at large. We see this most clearly when Eusebius of Caesarea defends Jesus Christ from the charge of being a mere sorcerer. Jesus, he insists, did not exploit His power; He did not use it to make women dependent on Him; He shunned the great cities in which He could have found an audience and built up a following; He was not a sorcerer, for He did not "meddle in everything and make Himself superior to other men . . . and claim ostentatiously that He possessed power that other men did not have." [63]

This sensitivity provided the *minus* side of a Late Antique man's mental graph of the impact of the supernatural on human affairs. The minus signs we might use, to the effect that certain claims or beliefs were "superstitious" or "irrational;" were frequently applied by groups that maintained securely vested traditions of learning, by doctors,[64] by legislators,[65] and by philosophers.[66] But though, for a modern man, such a minus might stand alone, even in learned circles there lay the additional, heavy weight of a specifically Late Antique man's minus: an acute awareness of the disruption and dominance within the group that might come from allowing a fellow member to wield new forms of power within it. To decide to allow a human being to exercise "heavenly" supernatural power involved something more than mere credulity. It meant moving slowly from the *minus* to the *plus* side of the graph. To decide that a man was a saint and not a sorcerer, the community had to overcome severe inhibitions and to release the well-tried defensive mechanisms with which ancient men were armed to hold new forms of supernatural power in check.

The antithesis of saint and sorcerer underlies much of Late Antique literature. Saints positively needed sorcerers. It is no coincidence that, at the moment when the primacy of St. Peter in the Roman church came to be most firmly established in the western Empire, in the early fifth century, the legend of his defeat of Simon Magus, "the other Simon," should have received wide currency.[67] Occasionally we can even catch a glimpse of a community in the act of making up its mind between the two. What is important for observers is not the fact of the power, but the way in which it is wielded and, above all, the stance which the wielder of this power took up to those who had benefited from it; as his friends told the king about Judas Thomas, he,

> was going about the cities and villages, and giving to the poor, and teaching them the new God, and also healing the sick and driving out demons, and doing many things; and we think that he is a sorcerer; but his compassion and his healing which he had done without recompense, make [us] think of him . . . that he is . . . an Apostle of the new God . . .; for he fasts much and prays much . . . and takes nothing from any man for himself.[68]

The assertion of the sovereignty of "good," "heavenly" power antithetical to, and often pitched in combat with, the "earthly" use of a supernatural power, which merely replicated in human society the tensions and anomalies of the invisible demonic society that crowded beneath the moon, was a theme that brought out the best in Late Antique authors. Eusebius' triumphant articulation of the monarchy of Christ,[69] Jamblichus' impassioned assertion of the sacramental unity of the *Cosmos*,[70] the astonishing Book Ten

of Augustine's *City of God*,[71] these are so many segments
of the arc of a great circle. The circle passed beyond books
into men's lives. The possibility of such ideas and of their
concrete embodiment in men and in institutions was discussed in a debate pieced together from the whole range of
what Late Antique men found acceptable and what repugnant
in the exercise of power in the world around them. This
process cannot be isolated as strictly religious; still less can
it be studied exclusively in terms of subjective shifts in men's
beliefs. Seemingly exotic and removed from the "realities"
of Roman social history, the study of demons and sorcerers,
of holy men and the modes of divine blessing in this world,
soon escapes the shelves of libraries. Nothing less is involved
in this debate than the changing quality of life and of social
relations in the Mediterranean world of the late second,
third, and fourth centuries.

It is for this reason that my starting point is the age of the
Antonines. At that time the individual wielder of supernatural power was still held in his place by firm restraints.
The towns of the Mediterranean had come to be firmly
controlled by small groupings of traditional families; and
the skill of such groups in influencing the religious as well
as the political climate of their locality was considerable.
The climate these fostered still favored the gods rather than
men. It placed its main emphasis on the direct, if spasmodic,
intervention of the gods by oracles and by dreams, which
still followed ancient precedents.[72] The claims of human
beings, and particularly of unaccustomed human beings, to
act as the permanent representatives of the gods were less in
evidence.[73] The continued power of oracles in the period
implied this. For in the traditional oracle, it was the god
alone who spoke: "Why need I enumerate all the wonderful
things that have been heard from the shrines themselves?
All the truths manifested to those who use victims and

sacrifices, and all those indicated by other incredible signs?
To some people there have been distinct appearances. The
whole of life is full of such appearances."[74]

An emphasis on the state of complete yet discontinuous
possession associated with oracles as a paradigm of human
contact with the divine flattened the profile of human intermediaries: the prophet was merely transparent to the god.
Even Alexander of Abonouteichos, hardly the most self-
effacing of prophets, thought it wise to split his business
with the traditional Clarian Apollo.[75] And even a figure who
intervened dramatically in public affairs as a magician, as did
the Egyptian Arnuphis in the campaigns of Marcus Aurelius,
did so as no more than the representative of the timeless
wisdom of his land.[76]

The image of the sorcerer lay to hand in all circles to cut
the exceptional and the threatening human being firmly
down to size. Accusations of sorcery flicker on the fringes of
the career even of Galen.[77] The magnificent Polemo knew
what language he could use of a rival:

> The man went round cities and their main squares gathering
> crowds . . . He was, above all, a very cunning magician, and
> declared that he could bring off great tricks, announcing that
> he could make the dead live. By these means, he gathered
> crowds of followers around him, men and women . . . He was a
> teacher of all ways of doing ill, and a collector of lethal drugs.[78]

The small-town community of Oea, in Tripolitania, used just
such accusations of sorcery to check the rise in their midst of
Apuleius, the Platonic philosopher;[79] and the Platonist
Celsus used the same to check the rise of Jesus Christ.[80]

On a different level, reading the *Meditations* of Marcus
Aurelius, one can appreciate that the experiences and the
attitudes against which he set his face already delineate with
uncanny fidelity the main features of Late Antique sensibility.
He is a man tensed against admitting those sharp moods,

moods of protest, of anger at existence, of amazement and high drama, that are so characteristic of Late Antiquity. The steady contemplation of the taut skein of a universe ruled by providence leaves, for him, no room for the starts and surprises that would accompany the work of human agents of the supernatural on earth. Exorcism, the Late Antique drama *par excellence*, by which the "heavenly" human being was seen to pit his power against the "earthly" forces of the demonic is placed, by Marcus Aurelius, among those trifles to which he had early learned to pay no heed, an equivalent of cockfighting.[81]

Yet the pressure of an alternative is there, in what men feel they now need to reject. Galen[82] and Lucian[83] discuss, if only to reject, the possibility of the *hyperanthrōpos*, the "superman," on earth. Lucian's mockery even throws the problem into high relief. His *bêtes noires* have a disturbingly Late Antique look about them, for he was already on the alert to attack individuals who pushed themselves forward in the name of a divine mission. This is what he stresses in their careers. We meet the Alexander who offered oracles from his own lips,[84] not the Alexander who continued to use his charisma to support belief in the traditional, impersonal oracle sites. We meet, in the egregious Peregrinus, the most faithful portrait of a second-century charismatic teacher in the Christian communities,[85] but not Peregrinus the civic benefactor.

This same Lucian, however, left us the portrait of Demonax. In Lucian's account all the tenderness and warmth of feeling that ancient men, classical and Late Antique alike, were capable of lavishing on a revered father figure wells up around this man.[86] As he walked the crowded streets of Athens, children would run up to him as to a father,[87] and his presence in a humble house brought the comfort and sense of security associated with a visitation of the gods.[88]

Looking at the age of the Antonines, we find that the role of the individual in relation to the divine is distinctly subdued. This is the impression we have from the great ornamental sarcophagi of Asia Minor: "We learn nothing of the individuality of the dead person. The carvings speak to us only of the distinguished, refined life-style and the classical culture of those who had themselves buried"[89] in such monuments. In the next century, the individual will leap into focus. Within a generation, portraits will appear on sarcophagi. By the middle of the third century, the portrait will have moved to a central position. The restless pageantry of classical mythology will come to rest around his grave figure and will be used to express his destiny and to clarify the nature of his links with heaven.[90] How, and against a background of what social changes, this development took place, will be the concern of the next two chapters.

2

AN AGE
OF AMBITION

It is difficult to start any narrative of a period of change
with a Golden Age, and all the more difficult when the alloy
of that gold is uncertain. Modern scholars are ill at ease
with the age of the Antonines. The splendid public manifestations of its cultural and religious life seem, at best, an
ominous lull before the storm and, at worst, contributory
factors to the breaking of the storm itself. Gibbon spoke of
it as an "age of indolence."[1] More recently, the impenitent
extroversion associated with the period has taken on a more
sinister look. The modern religious historian only too readily
regards an excess of public life as, in itself, a cause of emotional deprivation.

Thus, the late second century can be described as "patho-
logically traditionalist."[2] It is represented as an age whose
energies were wasted on externals: by trivialization, by
pedantry, by showmanship, the intellectual elites of the
Roman Empire had unwittingly sapped the resilience of the
rational tradition in classical scholarship and philosophy:
"L'éloquence atticisante des rhéteurs de la Nouvelle Sophis-
tique, imitée des grands anciens, rend un son creux. La
conférence publique où se délectent Pline le Jeune, Hérode

Atticus, Aristide, remplace le silencieux travail du vrai savant."[3] The revival of Atticism and of accompanying forms of idealization of the Greek past has been presented as an escape from reality.[4] These are heavy judgments for any age to bear. We do not like "the pretentious exponents of the renascent and now dominant Hellenic culture."[5] "Cerveaux vides et bouches sonores, pédants gonflés de vanité, et probablement malades imaginaires . . . Molière aurait eu plaisir à les rencontrer."[6] There is a feeling among scholars that such an age deserved Aelius Aristides[7] and that the neurotic need to depend on a divine protector that we choose to see in him is a neurosis that was fated to gather momentum in the coming century.[7]

This is one body of opinion from which I would wish to step aside in order to view the age of the Antonines from a different vantage point. I wish to bring it into relation with yet another body of opinion gathered around a set of phenomena which occurred a century later.

One singular merit, among so many, of Geffcken's *Ausgang des griechisch-römischen Heidentums* is that his profound epigraphic knowledge led him to assign a precise moment to the end of civic paganism. The inscriptions proclaiming public allegiance and whole-hearted private support to the cults of the traditional gods of the city, which had struck Geffcken as quite unexpectedly numerous in the late second and early third centuries, wither away within a generation after A.D. 260. The Tetrarchic age sees a brief, diminished, flare-up, and then the darkness descends forever on the gods.[8]

Ever since the appearance of Michael Rostovtzeff's *Social and Economic History of the Roman Empire*, this fact has been linked to the collapse of the traditional economic and social position of the cities in the Roman Empire in the course of the crisis of the third century.[9] If ever the death of a tradi-

tional religion in its public forms seems readily explicable ✓
in terms of the collapse of a traditional social order, then it is
in the death of classical paganism in the Mediterranean world
in the latter half of the third century.

I wish to step aside from this body of opinion also. We
know less than we once thought we knew about what
happened to urban life in the third century. We have come
to know far more than Rostovtzeff could have known about
the resilience and distinctive style of urban life in Late
Antiquity.[10] Careful study of the work of Libanius has
enabled us to see fourth-century Antioch as clearly as any
city of the classical Roman world.[11] Sensitive interpretation
of the excavations at Ostia and Djemila,[12] Sardis and
Ephesus,[13] have revealed to us Late Roman cities very
different from those of the age of the Antonines; but they are
not cities that have obligingly "laid them down and died."[14]
What were once taken for the death throes of city life in the
Roman Empire have come to appear as the growing pains by
which the Late Roman city replaced its classical predecessor.

Our view of the evolution of urban life in the third and
fourth centuries has become that much less simple. As a
result, the range of factors needed to explain the fate of
traditional urban religion and the rise of the Christian
church as an alternative to it, needs to become correspond-
ingly more differentiated. Bankruptcy and social collapse ✓
alone cannot explain the withering away of pagan inscriptions after A.D. 260. Nor can we be so certain that a clean
break lies between the late second and the late third centuries. The transformation of urban life in Late Antiquity
may have far deeper roots than we had thought. The civic
life of the age of the Antonines cannot be treated as a fixed
starting point. Its most skillful and sympathetic exponent,
Glen Bowersock, has made plain how the apparent stability
of the local patriotism of the age was no more than a moment

of delicate equipoise: "But—such is the nature of historical change—the coherence of the second century ὀικουμένη, which enabled the sophists to flourish, also allowed subsequent generations to pay more attention to Rome than to the cities from which they came."[15]

An awareness of how delicate the equipoise of the Antonine age was may lead us to a more sympathetic understanding of the religion and culture of those traditional families who set the tone in their cities. Features that have struck the historian as oppressively backward-looking or as dangerously superficial take on a different meaning if seen as devices for maintaining an equilibrium. Civic munificence, the studied revival of traditional collective cults and their accompanying ceremonies, emphasis on the commonplaces of classical culture—these were the governors of an engine that was in constant danger of overheating.

To understand how this should be and how it could change over a century we should look more closely into the ethos of city life in this period. As Ramsay MacMullen has reminded us: "The physical magnificence of imperial civilisation rested ultimately on sheer willingness."[16] Yet this sheer willingness was a complex phenomenon, to which a variety of factors contributed. When these factors combined, as they did in the age of the Antonines, willingness scattered the Empire with magniloquent inscriptions in praise of gods and men; when they fell apart, the willingness was redirected into other forms of expression—and the "gossiping stones" fall silent.[17]

We can come closer to the mainsprings of this willingness if we go to the most platitudinous of contemporaries. Apollonius of Tyana knew what civic life was all about: "He told them that for a city to be rightly conducted by its inhabitants, you need a mixture of concord with party spirit."[18] Let us explain the sage's paradox. He meant that strong competitive urges could be channeled into or at least palliated by attention to the collective life of the town. "*Philotimia*: No word understood to its depths goes further to explain the Greco-Roman achievement."[19] This was the driving force behind those more vague emotions—"patriotism," "archaism," "vanity"—that we ascribe to Antonine men. It had remained an explosive substance. On the one hand, it committed members of the upper class to a blatant competitiveness on all levels of social life. This was expressed with a candor and an abrasiveness peculiar to the society of the Roman Empire. Whatever reticence we may associate with the classical *polis* had long vanished.[20] On the other hand, the competitiveness of *philotimia* still assumed and needed, as it had done for centuries, an audience of significant others who were potential competitors. Without these the exercise of *philotimia* would have been deprived of a large part of its meaning. In such a context, Galen's rich man would move from stage to stage of his career, in each seeking out a peer group with whom he could meaningfully compare himself.[21]

Hence the paradoxical quality of the age of the Antonines and of the Severi. The phenomena that distinguished the society of the Later Empire—a sharpening of the division between the classes, the impoverishment of town councillors and the accumulation of wealth and status into ever fewer hands—were the most predictable developments in the social history of the Roman world. They were well under way by A.D. 200.[22]

Furthermore, in no part of the Empire had the politics of *philotimia* been free to develop in isolation. This is particularly true of the Greek east: the development of urban life from the classical into the Late Antique period can be documented there more clearly than elsewhere precisely because the urban upper classes had rapidly imposed their needs and their values on the central government of the Roman Empire and left an unparalleled abundance of evidence.[23] Plutarch complained, with complete justification, that the competitiveness of the urban magnates drew the imperial court and the Roman governing classes ever deeper into the politics of the Greek cities.[24] The very real possibilities of execution and confiscation by comparative outsiders added yet another risk to the game of forfeits that had always been the stuff of Greek life. A grandee such as Herodes Atticus found himself caught in distant Sirmium, on the Danubian frontier, between the Emperor Marcus Aurelius, the emperor's praetorian prefect, "Bassaeus, who was entrusted with the sword," and a delegation of his fellow Athenians, bent on ruining him with a charge of "tyranny."[25] It was an ugly moment. An almost identical scene was reenacted, two centuries later, on the same frontier, among the studiously ferocious Valentinian I, the grandee Petronius Probus, and a provincial delegation from Epirus.[26] In terms of the potential dangers of high politics, there was less to choose than we might suppose between the court of Marcus Aurelius and that of Valentinian I.

Of even greater long-term significance was the manner in which the overpowering weight of imperial patronage had already been thrown into one side of the balance of municipal status : " Yet there are others, Chians, Galatians or Bithynians, who are not content with whatever portion of either repute or power among their fellow-countrymen has fallen to their lot, but weep because they do not wear the patrician shoe."[27] Indeed, of all the developments in the social history of the Roman Empire, the process by which local families from the larger cities of the Greek East in the fourth century were drained upwards and away to the senate and court of Constantinople, leaving behind them a rump of resentful and vociferously impoverished colleagues, is the most predictable.[28] The more clearly this story emerges, as it now does from the dense pages of Fergus Millar's *The Emperor in the Roman World*, the less it is one which requires a dramatic "crisis" to explain it.

The fact that an image of monumental stability in the urban life of the age of the Antonines cannot serve as the starting point of any discussion of the "crisis" of the third century only serves to heighten the problems posed by the religious and cultural phenomena of the age. Faced by tensions that were clearly pulling the local community out of shape, urban elites all over the Empire appear to have strenuously mobilized the resources of their traditional culture, their traditional religious life, and for those who had good reason to afford it, their traditional standards of generosity in order to maintain some sense of communal solidarity. In this development, the exceptions prove the rule. The wide variety of urban life in the Empire, and the diverse evolutions of urban communities between the second and the fourth centuries, highlight the importance of cultural and religious factors. These were often decisive. Thus, along the Aegean coastline, where the inherited cultural and religious resources were most rich, local figures continued to maintain the traditional public life of the cities with deceptive ease and exuberance.[29] Other communities, such as the small, thinly Romanized society of Altava in Mauretania, lacked the religious and cultural resources with which to mask the naked facts of a "Late Roman" emergence to outright dominance of a small group of local landowners: as Pierre Pouthier observed, "Cette simplification hâtive du régime politique correspond à une absence de pénétration profonde de la religion romaine dans la cité."[30]

Peter Garnsey has written recently on the fate of the decurions, the average town councillors:

We are faced, therefore, with something of a paradox.
Detailed evidence has been presented which suggests that the
expenses of the decurionate were increasing by the first half
of the second century A.D., and that financial distress was not
absent from the ranks of the decurions. At the same time
inscriptions indicate that voluntary expenditure by local
benefactors reached a high point in quantity and value in the
same period.[31]

To explore this paradox may offer us a way into understanding the social changes of the third century as they
affected the public manifestations of traditional paganism.
At no time in the ancient world were the cultural and religious aspects of the public life of the towns mere trappings
which the urban elites could or could not afford, and which,
therefore, they found themselves forced to dispense with
after A.D. 260. This is too external a view of the linking of
religion and social life in the Roman world. Cultural and
social attitudes were intimately interwoven in the style of
urban life. For they were part of the complex mechanism
that had controlled the disruptive forces of *philotimia*. When
the style of life changed, these changed with it. The religious
and cultural history of the third and fourth centuries is
distinctive for that reason: to move from the age of the
Antonines to the age of Constantine is not to pass through
some moment of catastrophic breakdown, of bankruptcy,
depletion, pauperization, and the consequent "cutting back"
of expenditure on religious and cultural activity but rather
to pass from one dominant lifestyle, and its forms of expression, to another; to pass, in fact, from an age of equipoise to
an age of ambition.

The appeal of the age of the Antonines lies in the mobiliza-
tion of devices that blurred the hard edges of competitiveness and of widening social differentiation among the upper
classes of the cities of the Empire. It is, therefore, not too

paradoxical to see in the behavior of these groups of flamboyant and egotistical magnates the continuing pressure of a "model of parity." Elites tend to maintain a set of strong invisible boundaries, which mark firm upward limits to the aspirations of individuals, and to direct the aspirations of their members to forms of achievement that could potentially be shared by all other members in the peer group. In a — peer group, therefore, forms of individual achievement, like wealth, are there to be spent not hoarded. Those who accumulate too much to themselves are cut down to size in no uncertain manner, if not by the envoy of their fellows, then, at least, by the ineluctable envy of death. For Lucian, for instance, the anonymity of death was the most unanswerable rebuke to the claims of the superman.[32] Men committed to constant competition within a "model of parity" are not likely to allow any one of their peers to draw heavily on sources of power and prestige over which they have no control. Appeals to the other world as a source of special status in this world had to be kept within strictly conventional limits if they were to be acceptable. Plutarch knew what he was talking about when he dismissed those who, in order "to be reputed the favourites of heaven and above the common sort, invest their doings with a character of sanctity."[33]

The age of the Antonines is the last period of Mediterranean history before the Middle Ages when a "model of parity" and a stress on the community as a whole could be given full-blooded expression in terms of the ceremonies of the traditional religion. Put at its most material, to lavish funds on the public cults was a way of insuring oneself against envy and competition. The benefactor gave over wealth to the gods who, as invisible and immortal, stood for all that could be shared by the community. The formulae of the horoscopes reveal clearly what could be expected of an average career: "Then later, getting an inheritance and improving his means by shrewd enterprise, he became ambitious, dominant, munificent . . . and he provided temples and public works, and gained perpetual remembrance."[34] The reflex died hard. The successful alchemist in Byzantium knew as well as did any classical magnate in what form to pay his insurance premium for success: "A tenth part should go to the building of the holy churches and the care of the poor . . . so that he lives a life of a man of middling means and his practise shall be free of envy, and not be burdened with excessive wealth, eminence and expense."[35] Later still, in the fifteenth century, the rise to outright dominance of the Medici in Florence was cannily masked by the erection of vast Catholic shrines.[36] Such precautions were taken for granted in the second century A.D. Outstanding accumulations of wealth were best spent in this, studiously impersonal, manner—"on some occasion which offers a good and excellent pretext, one which is connected with the worship of a god or leads the people to piety."[37] We should not underestimate the effect of such gestures. They were less external than we might suppose; the public worship of the traditional gods still activated strong collective images of concord and parity, and firmly, if tacitly, excluded alternatives. We have seen how faith in the traditional oracles, for instance, condensed a particular way in which the divine made itself known to human beings: all men were equal in being equally passive to the spasmodic appearance of the gods in trance or dreams.[38]

In the Antonine age, these oracles had maintained their strong collective associations. They were valued because they could speak for the city as a whole on questions that affected the city as a whole. The Greek towns of the second century A.D. lived under the terror of earth tremors.[39] At such moments, the gods still spoke with confidence from their traditional sites; and they did so largely because they had been studiously maintained for that purpose by local benefactors. The Apollo of Patareia even broke his long silence after prolonged, and expensive, "nursing" by the generous Opromoas: and it was on the earthquake that he spoke.[40]

By such means, the ruling groups in the city were able to exercise a control of its religious life that went far deeper than mere display. It was they who interpreted the oracles. Eusebius (and Dr. Buresch) note drily that Apollo had come to speak an impressively good Greek.[41] By means of such oracles, disturbing novelties could be integrated into the traditional scheme of things. The Apollo of Didymai would relieve anxieties caused by a sequence of visions of the gods seen in unexpected forms by the inhabitants of Miletus.[42] With such oracles, any note of competitiveness was studiously avoided. The oracle of Apollo Kareios on the measures to be taken during a drought ends with "a dignified confession by the god that he does not know everything: it is not wise for a god to think he is cleverer than the other gods, or to enrich himself [?] on the strength of false claims."[43] Apollo Kareios knew what it was like to be a contemporary of Alexander of Abonouteichos.[44] Any up-to-date Apollo at Klaros could be trusted, in the third century, to give a reassuringly conventional opinion on the exact nature of the god Iao.[45]

Hence the crucial importance of the traditional oracles in the persecution of the Christians in the third century. The rise of Christianity and the final decline of paganism took place against a hubbub of speaking gods.[46] These oracles were not, as Christian apologists would have us believe, the isolated voices of defeated gods, nor were they merely the result of the machinations of frustrated priests. In the third century, at least, oracles against the Christians were merely an extreme application, to a dissenting religious group, of the day-to-day role of the oracle as the mouthpiece and the creator of public opinion, allaying anxiety, pinning blame,[47] offering reassurance in an old-fashioned tone of voice. Whenever the oracles speak out against the Christians in Late Antiquity, we can be sure that we are dealing with groups that can still find a collective voice; just as, when they fall silent, it is because a community has, somehow, lost its common language.

To create a culture where highly competitive men were, nonetheless, made constantly aware of what they shared with their peers and with their local communities, was the singular achievement of the Antonine age. The Atticizing revival and the consequent emphasis on a rhetorical training that drew its themes from a distant, admired past need not be seen as an escape from reality. It has been better interpreted as an attempt to create a common language in which all members of the upper class would share.[48] Reverence for the past had a practical role to play in the present. That acute observer of the human scene, Thomas Hobbes of Malmesbury, would have understood it only too well: "Particularly, competition of praise inclineth to a reverence of antiquity. For men contend with the living, not with the dead: to those ascribing more than due, that they may obscure the glory of the other."[49]

The discipline imposed on the elites of the Antonine age "model of parity" accounts for some of its best features. In the face-to-face society at the top of the cities, we are dealing with men who were acutely aware of the disruptive force of those styles of human relations that revealed too nakedly the brute facts of dominance and dependence in the Roman Empire. They put themselves out to avoid such tensions, at least among themselves. As Artemidorus of Daldis wrote: "Someone dreamt that he lifted up his clothes in front of his fellow members in an association to which he belonged and

urinated upon each of them. He was expelled from the
association as being unworthy of it . . . Someone dreamt that
he urinated in the middle of the theatre with the crowd
already seated . . . he showed contempt for the prevailing
laws just as he had also shown contempt for the spectators.
Nothing prevents magistrates, however," he is careful to add,
"from dreaming (in such a way) that they scorn their
subjects."[50] Ideals of unaffected friendship relations and of
power exercised without pomp and circumstance were
valued in the age of the Antonines, and they continued to
be cherished in many circles throughout Late Antiquity.[51]
They account for the charm of the Emperor Julian. For
Julian, to be a "Hellene" still imposed an attractive *sprez-
zatura*—the rejection in large, and often public, areas of his
life of all forms of affectation and formality.[52] It was a
rejection that was prized all the more in an age where the
maintenance of such old-fashioned standards of interpersonal
relations were known to be the sole surviving, silken thread
with which educated men hoped to bridle the raw human
nature of the governing classes of the Later Empire.[53]

Such sensitivity molded expectations of the way in which
men could relate to the divine. The men of the second
century continued the long debate on superstition. This was
not a debate about belief: it was a debate about the expression
of belief in human deportment. The superstitious man was
not the man who believed more firmly in the gods than any
others: he was the man who, in his relation to his invisible
neighbors, adopted stances that clashed with the ideal of
unaffected, unostentatious and unmanipulative relations
current among his visible neighbors.[54] The superstitious
man was like the sorcerer. He replicated in his relation to
the supernatural patterns of dominance and dependence that
were best left unexpressed.

The men of the Antonine age needed such disciplines.

In every age, a governing class thinks of itself as suffering from besetting weaknesses that are the antithesis and, maybe, the unwitting product of its dominant virtues. The besetting sin of the Antonine age is disquieting. Explosions of anger[55]—sudden fits that led to the biting, the kicking of dependents,[56] atoned for later by masochistic gestures[57]— these were the "illnesses of the soul" that Galen observed in his society as well as in his family. His father was the mildest of men, but his mother was a great biter.[50] The ferocity that we see unleashed in the vignettes of Ammianus Marcellinus of the governing class of the fourth century, plainly lurked beneath the more tranquil surface of Antonine life.

If the cultivated classes of the age had a problem, it lay in this static electricity of violence. Men were pushed by all the values of their environment into highly competitive stances: "Polemo went up to Dionysius, and leaning shoulder to shoulder with him, like those who begin a wrestling match . . . quoted 'Once, once they were strong, the men of Miletus.'"[59] The way in which such competitiveness could be shown was strictly curtailed. We can appreciate this if we turn to the dreams of the age, as these were written down and interpreted by contemporaries. We must read these with the eyes of second-century men. The dream did not merely reflect a state of mind: it was a private oracle. Thus, although the dreams that we have concern the individual destinies of men who hoped to achieve great things in their society, the manner in which their interpretation was made public by interpretation betrayed the same tacit pressures as those exerted by the traditional public oracles. The dream diviner puts two and two together in such a way as to assert a strong collective control of ambition.

The *Dream Book* of Artemidorus of Daldis takes us into a Mediterranean world where the common meanings that can be attached to dream images are well rooted and exceedingly matter-of-fact. Life is conceived of as a network of iron reciprocities which ends only in the *insouciance* of the grave: to give money to a beggar is a bad dream, for a beggar can give back as little as a corpse.[60] In such a life, expectations are held within firm limits. Those who would draw from dream images conclusions that might foster extremes of exaltation or humility receive no encouragement from Artemidorus. To dream that one is a suckling child—a dream which later ages would treat as an image of tender care and a source of inspiration (one thinks of Fulbert of Chartres who derived his wisdom from being suckled by the Virgin)—merely relived, for Artemidorus, the impotence of childhood. It was a dream that portended poverty and resentful dependence.[61] Dreams of exaltation also awakened his suspicion. To fly in one's home town meant that you may not put foot in it again.[62] To dream that you were larger than life boded no good.[63] For a poor man to dream that he had a crown was a bad sign—"for it was contrary to his status";[64] and the fate of contemporary Christian martyrs would have proved the prognosis only too right.

It is against this background that we must touch on our best-known dreamer, Aelius Aristides. I am reluctant to do so. The poor man has had to bear far too heavy a weight of *odium psychologicum* from modern scholars.[65] The problem of Aristides lies mainly with ourselves. He puzzles us; and it is this puzzlement which has forced so many scholars into precipitate psychiatric judgment on him. We obscurely resent the fact that a degree of intimacy with the divine which would make a saint or a martyr of any of us should merely serve to produce a hypochondriacal gentleman of indomitable will. We judge him, in fact, by Late Antique standards. We expect contact with the divine to be used on earth in a more drastic manner. But Aristides' dreams are consonant with the whole "style" of the religious life of his peers. Men like Aristides, like Apuleius,[66] like Apuleius' Lucius[67] were able to strike up a permanent, nourishing relationship with stable ideal figures; but they expected this relationship to help them through a life whose forms and expectations were laid down for them in frankly this-worldly terms. To draw on such a relationship for any other purpose would be to opt out from their audience of significant others, by stressing this one relationship with an invisible figure at the expense of the network of relationships that they shared with a visible circle of friends and competitors against the well-known backdrop of their cities.

Aelius Aristides, therefore, was caught on a knife-edge by the demands of a model of parity. He was free to make full use of his relationship with Asclepius in claiming to be superior to his fellows. With deliberate showmanship, he followed up a reference to the superiority conferred by his intimate relationship to the god—taken from a dream recorded in the *Sacred Tales* and used by him in a public speech in praise of Asclepius—to write yet another speech, "On why I dropped that clanger."[68] This was a tract in favor of boasting and in favor of the superiority which some men drew from their relationship with invisible guides and protectors. The *daimon* of Socrates received due prominence: "I tell you, Socrates spent the whole of his life vaunting his superiority."[69] All this was allowed to Aristides, as to any of his contemporaries. It is the world of Polemo, who "conversed with cities as inferiors, Emperors as not superiors, and gods as equals."[70] Yet, *verba volant*: "vaunting," though encouraged by century-old traditions, was bridled by equally firm controls. Superiority was not to be impetuously translated into action, in the form of radical departures from the prevailing lifestyle of one's peers.

Here, perhaps, Aristides was made to pay a heavy price

for his divine blessing. Both he and his contemporaries realized that what made him superior appeared to come from no choice of his own—it was the crippling regime of the invalid.[71] It might be worth our while to inquire why this should be so. Asclepius, as Galen realized, dealt with his patients at the level of their "heat." In ancient medicine, this was as pervasive and as intangible a force as the instinctual life of the modern unconscious. It was in this "heat" that the pent-up energies, whose public expression so disturbed Galen, resided. Asclepius, in Galen's opinion, was the only doctor who, by virtue of his contact with the patient in his dreams, could provide innocent if peculiar means of bringing their "heat" safely to the boil.[72] Aristides had his fair share of "heat." So many of the more flamboyant actions prescribed to him by Asclepius either put this "heat" on its mettle by surviving plunges into icy water[73] or discharged it in unaccustomed activity.[74]

Aristides' behavior, therefore, poses a problem: did the rising within him of a threatening sense of superiority backed by considerable energy and aggression unconsciously help bring on the illnesses and the murderous cures that tied his energy down to a battle with his body, so that Aristides' overweening ambition was safely locked away in a world of grandiose dreams and visions? This seems to be the case. Only in that drastic way could he control his "heat," as Galen describes it in others. Aristides gives the impression of a powerful engine constantly stalling through being driven on the brake. What he may have lacked was what contemporaries of other classes and regions were groping toward in their radical religious beliefs: a religious means of expressing, by drastic gestures of protest or renunciation, such as the publicizing of visions to their fellow believers or the adoption of harsh regimes of fasting and the avoidance of care for the body, that sense of separateness which went with a sense of superiority based upon closeness to the divine. Tertullian, for instance, shared to a great extent in the same culture as Aristides. Yet, only a generation later he had found his way, through the Christian "prophetism" of the Montanists, to a group that acted out the issues with which Aristides had grappled on his sick bed.

Aristides, by contrast, would never let his intimacy with Asclepius pass beyond the bounds laid down by Antonine convention. The earthquake of September 149 activated the the traditional religious procedures of Ephesus and Smyrna: "And on the one hand, they sent emissaries to Claros, and the oracle was fought about, and, on the other, holding olive branches of supplication, they went about the altars and the market place and the circuit of the city."[75] Yet Aristides was convinced that it was his private sacrifice that had brought safety to the city: "I intended to say that there is no need to be afraid, for there would be nothing harmful . . . Then I stopped, so that I might not seem to be some demagogue."[76] To keep such knowledge to oneself, for such reasons, may be as damaging to health and sanity as to have it in the first place.

It is the same with his lifestyle. Had we met Aristides in 171, we would have found him as unwashed, for the past five years, as any later Christian hermit: he had been in the grip of an obsession about avoiding baths.[77] An image of the body that formed part of the Mediterranean *koiné* of the age regarded the avoidance of water on its surfaces as a means of rendering the body "dry," crisp, and light, and so the fit vehicle of a soul freed of its heavy, "earthly" elements.[78] Tertullian, for instance, justified the "dry" fasting of his Montanist fellow believers in those terms. Such an image may have lurked at the back of Aristides' mind, but he refused to draw on the power of the symbol in making sense of his own regime. For many of his contemporaries, the "dryness" of an unwashed body had become a statement, which a religious group could acclaim, of a separateness and a superiority that betrayed a "heavenly" origin.[79] For Aristides, the nagging question of "to bathe or not to bathe" remained private; and his rejection of baths remained locked away in the labyrinthine courses of his illness.

It is only possible to touch on this aspect of the Antonine age with the tips of one's fingers: to weigh any more heavily on it would be to score a cheap triumph of modern clinical knowingness at the expense of the dead. If it is legitimate, as I suggest it might be, to use the life of Aelius Aristides to sense the inner tensions of a particular group at a particular time, then I would suggest that the tension lies in the area for which we have the evidence: in the combination of exalted dreams with a matter-of-fact, even a curtailed, lifestyle.

Such restraints on ambition, however, did not last for much longer in the Roman world. The flowering of urban life in the Antonine age is usually thought of as an Indian summer. The image is misleading; for it assumes that the golden autumn leaves were brought to the ground by winds that came from corners of the world distant from the cities—that, in the third century, the imperial court, the imperial administration and the army were forces that came to impinge from the outside on the life of the traditional urban classes. This is far from being the case. The style of urban life I have been describing was like a set of beams held horizontally by strong, head-on pressures: at a touch, they would spring upwards and apart. In the third century, the life of the upper classes of the Roman world did not collapse under pressure outside: it exploded.

The experience of the Roman Empire in the "crisis" of the third century is not so very different from what we find in any other aristocratic society passing through a period of uncertain government—the situation led to an escalation of feuds. Wherever we find the evidence, we find the cities and the provincial aristocracies in a scramble of competition—city against city in Asia Minor,[80] great landowner against great landowner, as in Capellianus' suppression of the revolt of the Gordians in North Africa.[81] The "sheer willingness" of *philotimia* came to wear a more unpleasant face through being now openly joined to armed force; but the language remained the same. The army had merely joined the significant others before whom *philotimia* had to be shown: emperors who could not keep up the pace came to grief.[82] Those clear-eyed observers of the third century scene, the rabbis, were right to see in the usurping emperor no more than the urban *philotimos* writ large: "It can be compared to a king who enters into the state . . . What did he do? He built walls for them. He brought water for them. He fought their wars. He said to them: 'I will rule over you.' They said: 'Yes, yes.'"[83] The militarization of the Empire, therefore, was not a phenomenon that took place in isolation: it was part of a general unleashing of competitive urges.

Nor should we think of the changes in the structure of status in the local communities as something imposed upon them entirely from the outside. Increased taxation and the consequent increase in administrative responsibilities merely opened yet further avenues for competition. The notables in towns along the military highways of Rough Cilicia, for instance, who came to insert into their traditional catalogue of civic honors the frequent accompanying of the *annona* "to the divine camps,"[84] may not have viewed the process with the same dismay as does a modern historian of the relation of city and imperial administration. The "pyramidal" hierarchy of the Later Empire grew from the ground up. It was not brought about by some profound dislocation, or by the intrusion of an alien force. It was the natural way in which a governing class, which had been committed for generations to competition in power, honor, and reputation, regrouped itself in an age where the rewards of such competition, for the successful few, appeared greater than ever before. What collapsed, therefore, in the course of the third century, were not the urban aristocracies as such, but rather the mechanisms by which they had channeled their more disruptive ambitions into their cities and had veiled their successes with old-fashioned decencies.

Our impression of the distress and confusion of the age arises, in fact, from the slow emergence of clarity. Awkward compromises break down. The changing tone of imperial letters show this. That of Gordian III to Aphrodisias in Caria can still avoid a *de haut en bas* tone: it speaks of Aphrodisias as "your city" and Rome as "my city."[85] The letter of Gallienus on the rights of the *metropolis* over against other towns already betrays incoherence: "The stilted style and high moral tone shows that our edict is well on the way to the age of Diocletian, but what is different is the almost anxious argumentative manner and the wheedling friendliness."[86] In an inscription on the same topic from the reign of Valens, a century later, the incoherence is at an end. The situation is made brutally plain. There are a few big cities and many smaller cities:[87] those "whose souls embrace the wish for popular acclaim" may do so in the *metropolis* but only after they have performed their obligations in their smaller home towns.[88] The one thing that a fourth-century *curialis* never lacked was blunt certainty as to what he was expected to do, and a clear view of the ladder of status that he might, or might not, be allowed to scale.[89] There is little room in fourth-century rulings for the unspoken balances and official reticence of an earlier age.

Indeed, the attraction of the reign of Diocletian lies partly in its certainty of touch and its explicitness. Diocletian and his advisers appear to have had no hesitation in calling a spade a spade.[90] This was all the more convincing for still being couched in resolutely traditional terms. In the late third century, lawyers, administrators, and panegyrists found themselves building new, clear structures out of ancient materials they already knew how to handle—a good basis for quick, firm work.[91]

The contours of the new situation were unmistakable and are well known. "Soft" government was replaced by "hard" government.[92] The emperors of the second century had ruled the Mediterranean with "magnificent economy of effort,"[93] through a tacit collusion with the upper classes of the cities. "The one sure maxim of extended Empire, a wise and salutary neglect," had kept the impingement of taxation and of the direct representatives of the state at a very low level in comparison with the Later Empire. This had left the traditional mechanisms sufficiently intact to transmute *philotimia* into "sheer willingness" in its most acceptable and traditional form, "with piety towards the gods, and generosity towards men."[94]

A system of "hard" government depleted these mechanisms. The collaborators came to identify their status and power with the position they enjoyed in the imperial government. The delicate balance implied in innumerable inscriptions of the second and early third centuries—"friend of the Emperor, friend of the home-town, friend of [its] gods"—was irreversibly upset.[95] Whether it was exercised benignly as *patrocinium*, or abrasively as *potentia*, this power drew its *raison d'être* from beyond the local community. Its more exalted source made it that much less vulnerable to local pressure; and the power itself—which manipulated a system of taxation and of punishment that had increased in weight—could win out in a more unambiguous manner. A fourth-century *potens* did not have to pay the insurance premiums for success which his more evenly balanced predecessors of the second century had done. If he did, he paid them in a different currency, which we do not recognize so easily.

The Late Antique city, therefore, was neither impover- ished, nor was it devoid of ceremony. Wealth and ceremonial had merely drained away from its former vehicles, the public buildings and the public cults. This was shown in the urban landscape. The glory of a Late Antique town lay in its private palaces. These dominated the city. Often, as in Ostia and Djemila, they pushed the traditional public thoroughfares out of shape.[96] The palace of Majorinus—the seat of a family whose status was intimately connected with the new patterns of dominance—was one of the sights of Antioch: it is shown on the Yakto mosaic of the fifth century on the same footing as the public buildings.[97] Such great palaces had a permanence which the give-and-take of second-century public displays deliberately avoided. Their magnificence spoke more eloquently and more enduringly of the status of the owner and his family than did the "gossiping stones" of a previous age. In the west, the Late Antique town was devoured by its private buildings. By the early sixth century, the civic facade of the Italian towns was maintained through the deliberate appropriation of public buildings by private owners: in private hands, at least, they would not diminish the glory of the city . . . by falling down.[98]

The ceremonial life of the town, also, shifted in a manner that hints at one of the most puzzling and elusive evolutions in the Late Antique period. So much emphasis has been placed on the withering away of the traditional means by which classical paganism had been expressed, that the new means by which paganism—or, at least, non-Christianity—continued to be rendered visible in public, but in a new idiom, have received far less attention. By assuming that paganism withered away, and that it was immediately replaced by

Christianity, we ignore a large, and fascinating, tract of Late Roman religious life: paganism was transformed by being linked to a new ceremonial of power.

In the course of the fourth century, the traditional associations of pagan worship were abandoned—sacrifice and temples. What survives is a groundswell of pagan religiosity that was impenitently soundproof to Christianity—divine figures who had lost little of their numinous power through losing their sacrifices, and ceremonies that spoke of the basic rhythms of Mediterranean life no less clearly for avoiding the temples.

A generation after public paganism appeared to have ebbed from the cities, the feast of the Kalends of January—a feast which had been limited to Rome in the High Empire—spread throughout the Mediterranean. Linked to the entry into office of the consuls, associated with the *salutationes* and gift giving that had always linked the *patronus* to his clients, it was a feast of men not of gods, and of men entering unashamedly into the fruits of power and prosperity. It was the ceremony *par excellence* of an age of ambition; and it lasted through the centuries, to disturb the Christian bishops with annual reminders of the natural man and his aspirations, cut loose from the reticences of an earlier age and splendidly untinctured by the new faith.[99]

It is against this background that we can appreciate the dilemmas of the upholders of public pagan worship in the early fourth century. They were dealing with a world that had not been crippled; but it had lost its balance.

The Tetrarchy offered a new equipoise around the person of the emperor. The identification of the piety of the emperor with the safety of the state is an ancient theme, one that reached back beyond Augustus.[100] There was, therefore, nothing new, much less artificial, about Diocletian's solemn consultation of the oracles before the persecution of the

Christians[101] or in his linking of himself with the traditional cults in monuments as far apart as Rome, Thessalonica, and Ephesus.[102] What was lacking, however, was the seemingly unflagging zeal with which members of the local community collaborated with such displays. Even in Ephesus, a renewal of collective memories of the deeds of Artemis for her city, in the form of new carvings on the facade of the Hadrianic temple, hung on the thread of the imperial cult, whose statues stood at its foot.[103] The emperor alone was the *laetitiae publicae | caerimoniarumque | omnium autor(i)*.[104] The revival of a civic oracle in Antioch, by an imperial official, merely ended in a sorcery purge quite as ugly as any that would happen in the same city under a Christian emperor: excessive initiative, even against the enemies of the gods of a pagan Empire, was dangerous.[105]

As a result, we find that public paganism survives only in those cites where the local *potentes* were sufficiently firmly in the saddle to continue to use it as before. The third century, as we know it, does not appear to have happened in Stratonikeia.[106] No sooner had the light of the emperor's arrival "shone down" on the city, between 305 and 313, than the ancient mechanisms revived: the statue of Marcus Sempronius Arruntius Theodotus was set up in the Stoa his father had built, beside that of his great grandfather.[107] This is a family so firmly ensconced as to need little encouragement to show its outright power in the locality in the old-fashioned manner.

The same happened in Athens, but with a significant difference. The social structure of the city shows an impressive continuity;[108] but the tone of Athenian paganism moved with the times. Athens became a town "Where Cabots speak only to Lowells, and Lowells speak only to God." An esoteric paganism, such as might have brought down on the heads of its practitioners in earlier times an accusation of sorcery or of demagoguery was accepted as the basis of the continued predominance of intellectual elites in Athens and in other cities of the Aegean.[109] Collective support for the pagan cults, however, rallied with as much difficulty in Athens as elsewhere. This is a scene from two centuries after Aristides:

> Further, earthquakes occurred in some places: Crete was shaken rather violently, as were the Peloponnesus and the rest of Greece, where several cities tottered outside of Athens and Attica; these last according to report were spared as follows. Nestorius, who was at the time hierophant, had a dream prescribing that the hero Achilles should be honored with public honors, which would prove the salvation of the city. When he imparted this dream to the magistrates, they thought him delirious (he was already a decrepit old man) and accounted as nothing what he had told them. He then deliberated with himself, schooled as he was in divine doctrine, as to what should be done. Having fashioned in his tiny house an image of the hero, he placed it below the cult-statue of Athena Parthenos. And, as often as he performed the customary rites sacred to the goddess, at one and the same time he performed those which he knew had been ordained for the hero. Thus did he fulfill the counsel of his dream and, when the earthquake hit, the Athenians alone, as it happened, were saved, all Attica as well sharing in the hero's benefactions. That this story is true may be learned from the memoirs of the philosopher Syrianus.[110]

The evolution we have sketched out in a few tentative strokes lies behind the failure of Julian. In a great city such as Antioch, the ceremonial of the *potentes* had come to mean more than the ceremonies of the gods. Julian had given funds to the city for collective sacrifice: "Accordingly, I hastened thither . . . thinking that I should enjoy the sight of your wealth and public spirit. And I imagined . . . the sort of procession it would be . . . beasts for sacrifice, libations, choirs in honor of the gods, incense and the youth of the city surrounding the shrine."[111] But when he arrived, he found an old priest and his goose. The Antiochenes had spent the money on chariot racing. They had invested in that ceremonial of power and good fortune in which the cities of the eastern Empire crystallized a new, more secular, sense of stability and triumph.[112] On such occasions they would have witnessed the last flowering of the urban benefactor, now dominant as the *patronus* and the *potens*. John Chrysostom's congregation had seen him:

> The theatre is filling up, all the people are sitting aloft presenting a splendid sight, composed of numberless faces. Then, as the public figure who has brought them together enters, they all stand up and chant unanimously. All with one voice they acclaim him "Protector," "Ruler" of their common city; they stretch out their hands in salutes . . . They hail him as "The Nile of Gifts," "The Ocean."[113]

By the reign of Theodosius II this ceremonial of power would focus on the *potens par excellence* of Byzantium—the emperor himself. The defeat of Julian at Antioch was not a victory of the Christian church. It was the victory of a Late Antique mentality and style of life that would blossom, in a hauntingly non-Christian form, in the ceremonial of the Hippodrome of Constantinople.[114]

3

THE RISE
OF THE
FRIENDS OF GOD

Aelius Aristides was not the only man in the second century A.D. to find himself on a country estate with time on his hands, and to fall to dreaming. But the dreams of the others were of more drastic practical relevance. Polycarp, for instance, a Christian bishop waiting the turn of events at his farm outside Smyrna, "fell into a trance while at prayer: he saw his pillow being consumed by fire. He turned and said to his companions: 'I am to be burned alive.'"[1] The best part of a century later Cyprian, bishop of Carthage, in retirement at Curubis, saw the proconsul sentence him in a wordless dream: the dumb show of the dream revealed to him that he had exactly a year in which to put in order the affairs of his church.[2]

These dreamers would impinge on the public. Crowds gathered for a distribution of largesse by an urban notable might be prepared to exclaim "Great is Asclepius" at the sight of a pink professor emerging from his mid-winter plunge into the swollen river, insensitive, as in a visionary trance, to the rigors of his strange regime.[3] Crowds, in a less favorable mood, would also watch men and women, similarly wrapt in a vision, treading the icy river of death.

Those who grouped themselves around such public dreamers had invested them with a heady enthusiasm: "Polycarp took off all his clothing, loosed his belt and even tried to take off his own sandals, although he had never had to do this before: for all the Christians were always eager to be the first to touch his flesh."[4] Their perception of the grim scene of public burning that followed differed from the normal. When Lucian was present at the self-immolation of Peregrinus he remarked, "It is not an agreeable spectacle to look at an old man who has been roasted, getting our nostrils filled with a villainous reek."[5] The death of Polycarp was attended by a sweet smell of perfume, a mixture of all that was most exquisite and ideal in the Mediterranean world with the solemnity of the Old Testament burnt offering.[6]

The urban notables were taking no risks with such a figure. Nicetes, father of the current eirenarch, "prevented us even from taking up the poor body, though so many were eager to do so and to have a share in his holy flesh . . . 'Otherwise,' he said, 'they may abandon the Crucified and begin to worship this man.'"[7]

It is from small details such as these, preserved in the *Acts of the Martyrs*, that we can sense the strains to which the skillfully orchestrated equipoise of the cities of the Antonine and Severan ages had come to be subjected. The martyrs were not merely protestors against conventional religion, nor were they particularly noteworthy as men and women who faced execution with unusual courage: as the notables of Smyrna told a later bishop, they were too used to professional stars of violence—to gladiators and beast hunters—to be unduly impressed by those who made a performance out of making light of death.[8] Rather, the martyrs stood for a particular style of religious experience. "The primitive Christians," wrote Gibbon, "perpetually trod on mystic ground."[9] The Christians admired their martyrs because they had made themselves the "friends of God"; they summed up in their persons the aspirations of a group made separate from, and far superior to, their fellow men by reason of a special intimacy with the divine.

The rise of the Christian church in the late second and third centuries is the rise of a body of men led by self-styled "friends of God," who claimed to have found dominance over the "earthly" forces of their world through a special relation to heaven. The *Acts of the Martyrs* stressed this aspect of the experiences of their heroes. Friendship with God raised the Christians above the identity they shared with their fellows. The *nomen Christianum* they flaunted was a "non-name." It excluded the current names of kin and township and pointed deliberately to a widening hole in the network of social relations by which other inhabitants of the Roman towns were still content to establish their identity: "He resisted them with such determination that he would not even tell them his own name, his race, or the city he was from, whether he was a slave or a freedman. To all their questions he answered in Latin: 'I am a Christian!'"[10]

The heroism of the martyrs was merely the climax of the inherent sense of superiority of the Christians as a whole. Such heroism was far more than a triumph of purely human courage. The pain of martyrdom was thought of as irrelevant to a human body that had already turned away in trance from the ties of its human environment and was wrapped in close intimacy with Christ: "The Lord stood by them in a vision and spoke with them."[11] The martyrs threatened to bring the other world into this world in no uncertain manner. It is hardly surprising that the well-tried defensive mechanisms of Mediterranean men were mobilized against them. Their claims to supernatural power were "contained," not denied, by accusations of sorcery.[12] Reverence for the martyrs was rendered sinister by emphasis on the uncanny and the undesirable associations of the graves of those who had died a violent death.[13]

In the late second and third centuries, the Christians became figures to be reckoned with in the Roman world. They did so largely because they had a singularly articulate and radical contribution to make to that great debate, whose outlines were sketched in the first chapter, on the manner in which supernatural power could be exercised in society. The way in which the Christians idealized their martyrs as the special "friends of God," and the manner in which they organized themselves around bishops who claimed with increasing assertiveness to be "friends of God" in a similar manner, condensed the main issues of that debate. In following through this theme, we can make some sense of the tantalizing evidence for the position of the Christian church in the Mediterranean world in the century before the conversion of Constantine.

Far less than we might wish can be said with certainty about the pre-Constantinian church. Its numbers and rate of expansion are likely to remain forever obscure. There is even much to be said for not regarding the rate of expansion of Christianity in this period as the most significant feature of its position in Roman society. How the Christians thought about themselves is what we can know; and it may well be that the way in which they articulated their attitude to themselves and to the outside world counted for more than spectacular or massive conversions. That Christian bishops could explain to Constantine why he had been converted to Christianity was more important for the long-term fortunes of their church than the opaque fact of the conversion itself.

Beyond this, modern knowledge can do no more than set the historical imagination free from stereotypes. What facts we can know, we have already known for a long time: A clear picture of the social and cultural "scatter" of

Christianity in the third century has long been available in Adolf von Harnack's *Mission und Ausbreitung des Christentums*.[14] What we still lack is a social and cultural history of the third-century Roman Empire that can make the unexpected elements in this "scatter" a little more intelligible and so more credible.

The Christian church was plainly more complex and more rich in economic[15] and intellectual resources than the stereotype of uneducated artisans and silly women[16] that was presented at the time by pagan polemic and that modern myth has transmuted into a heroic band of outcasts. Such a stereotype does not fit writers like Tertullian[17] nor bishops like Callistus,[18] Cyprian,[19] and Paul of Samosata.[20] Even in a village near Oxyrhynchus, a Christian church had doors of bronze substantial enough to be confiscated and transported all the way to Alexandria in 303.[21]

Compared with these tantalizing glimpses, glimpses that stretch the historical imagination rather than satisfy it, the theme of the rise of the "friends of God" has the merit of being fully documented, in both pagan and Christian sources. Furthermore, it has the great advantage of presenting the inner dimensions of the problem. In the shifting emphases of Christian writers, we can glimpse a debate, passing from generation to generation by means of subtle adjustments in the *koiné* of ancient religious experience, as to the modes of human contact with the divine and so to the applicability of such contact within the human community.

The evolution was all the more significant for forming a part of a tide that was flowing in the pagan world also. It was all the more crucial, in its immediate social impact, for reflecting with great sensitivity the concomitant changes in the structure of the Mediterranean towns. A growing certainty that "friends of God" could exist and could be seen to exist in this world and that their friendship with God entitled them to considerable and permanent powers over their neighbors becomes ever more clear from the mid-third century onwards. At just this period, the equipoise of the Antonine age collapsed. At a time when the "model of parity" was sapped by the tendency of a few members of the local community to enjoy a privileged status at the expense of their fellows, religious leaders emerged, and were encouraged to emerge, in pagan and Christian circles alike, who were prepared to stand out from their fellows in a far more blatant eminence than previously. By the end of the third century, Roman society did not have to reckon with one high-pitched hierarchy alone. Over against the secular hierarchy of an increasingly "pyramidal" society there stood, in clear outline, a spiritual hierarchy of "friends of God," the source and legitimacy of their power in this world held to rest unambiguously on a heavenly origin.

In the mid-third century, we see in Cyprian of Carthage an urban notable able to gather around himself a permanent residue of prestige, which, as a martyr bishop, he would take care to bequeath to his considerable following.

Late in the century, in the circles of Plotinus, of Porphyry, and in the early fourth century, with Jamblichus, the image of the "divine man" takes on firmer outlines among pagan philosophers. The appearance within one generation of two major lives of Pythagoras is the symptom of this change. It is a change that would have annoyed Lucian: for in his *Bazaar of Philosophers*, the Pythagoreans had stood out as the sellers of supernatural snobbery; they had offered "the superior life," "the most majestic," the way to become a superman.[22] By the late third century, such ambitions had come to be wholeheartedly accepted.

The problem that faced the pagan thinkers in Late Antiquity was how to allow such a "divine man" to emerge to outright eminence, shorn of the ambivalences traditionally associated with the average exercise of supernatural power. The rise of the pagan "friend of God" was less straightforward than it had been in a Christian environment. Yet it reflects, all the more faithfully for being more cautious, the way in which groups in Late Antiquity made up their mind to acclaim some of their members as the wielders of unambiguous "heavenly" power. The pagan biographical tradition, therefore, forms a doublet to the main theme of this chapter.

⟨ Pagan literature of the fourth and fifth centuries became more preoccupied than ever previously with the delicate watershed between "heavenly" and "earthly" forms of supernatural power and with which types of individual derived their position in society from which sources. As a result of this preoccupation, the "saint" and the "sorcerer" appear uncomfortably close together in contemporary accounts of neo-Platonic circles. It is only too easy for the modern scholar to dismiss such circles as having blurred the boundaries between magic and philosophy. To do this is to import modern criteria into a peculiarly Late Antique debate, and so to miss its point. For the distinction between rational philosophy and irrational magic, though present, was never central to the debate. What was hotly debated was the difference between legitimate and illegitimate forms of supernatural power. This was a boundary which Late Antique pagans had learned to scan with alert eyes and firm criteria. Their cosmic beliefs mirrored and made articulate implicit assumptions as to how men were supposed to exercise power and influence among their fellows. Some were thought to draw their power from tranquil and unmanipulative contact with the higher orders of the invisible universe; others could be "led astray into the exercise of earthly and material powers." [23]

Thus, Jamblichus' intervention in favor of theurgic rites meant far more than the reception by sophisticated intellectuals of irrational magical practices. From Jamblichus' point of view, it was the other way around. He wished to put his finger on a secure *locus* of the supernatural where his opponent Porphyry had seen only the quicksands of manipulative sorcery. In *On the Mysteries of Egypt* he wished to fight a *cause célèbre* so as to ensure that a wide range of priestly actions and of traditional divination, as practiced by himself and his fellows, could be treated as raised definitely above the ambiguities of magic and trance. Jamblichus' sacramental theory represents an attempt to draw the line that linked the pagan "friend of God" to heaven in such a way that it would stand out clear and straight, unsmudged by being confused with the "earthly" practices of the common sorcerer.[24]

Looking back a century later, Eunapius of Sardis drew up his gallery of pagan philosophers according to similar criteria. He is not greatly concerned, as modern scholars have been, to decide who among these was the more or the less "rational." Moving as he did in a distinctive social world, among the well-to-do, well-educated gentlefolk of the cities of the Aegean, Eunapius is always on the alert as to who, among a group of potential peers, were "pushers" and who had played out their roles in an unhurried and traditional manner. "Sorcerer" and "saint" lay one to each side of that watershed of social behavior. On the one side, therefore, we find Maximus of Ephesus, the notorious mentor of the Emperor Julian. For Eunapius he is an impressive and meteoric figure. But his behavior with the gods was all of a piece with his behavior to his fellow men: with both, he had pushed his luck. In his relations with oracles and seances he had not been a charlatan—only a man in too great a hurry. He was the paradigm of the man of "skill and daring."[25] By contrast, Eunapius wholeheartedly admired Aedesius. For here was a figure whose relationship with the gods was

exemplary because utterly secure: "His kinship and affinity
with the gods was so unceremonious and familiar that he
had only to place the garland on his head and turn his gaze
upwards to the sun, and immediately deliver oracles which,
moreover, were always infallible and were composed after
the fairest models of divine inspiration."[26] In Eunapius'
Lives of the Sophists, therefore, we meet something more
revealing than so many vignettes from which modern scholars
can register the ravages of the irrational among remote and
ineffectual dons. We can sense in even the most eccentric of
his portraits the sustained efforts of a group to find figures
that they could admire as an oasis of certainty in a world
shot through with ambition.

— Pagan intellectuals of the late third and fourth centuries
moved more hesitantly than had their more radical Christian
counterparts toward the acceptance of unalloyed hero worship
and its corollary, the exclusive dominance of the "saint"
over the "sorcerer." There is still room in Eunapius' world
for a Maximus of Ephesus, flawed though he might be. With
the conversion of Constantine to Christianity, by contrast,
the Christian church showed how rapidly it had moved in
the generations when pagan philosophers had only begun to
grope for a stable image of the "divine man." For, in the
official recognition and the immediate granting of massive
privileges to the Christian church, two sides of the arch of
Late Antique social and religious developments joined
ostentatiously in the person of Constantine. Constantine
was an autocrat, an explicit articulator of the high-pitched
society of the later Roman Empire; and in his relations with
the Christian church, he shared with his coreligionists the
belief their leaders had come to foster so skillfully for themselves— a belief that the protection and the inspiration on
which a "friend of God" might draw could be applied to
teaching, to decision making, to the control and concord of

large communities, and need not be used only to face death. Constantine was not a man to be outdone in matters of *Religionsgeschichte*. Though they receive great prominence in modern scholarship, the visions that accompanied his conversion in 312 were no more than passing incidents in a lifelong style of relationship with the supernatural: as befitted a "friend of God," he was recipient of ten thousand such heartening visitations.

The theory [that the Emperor enjoyed the special protection of a god] is introduced from political motives in all probability, to raise the emperor above the arbitrary whim of the praetorians. But its persistence is due to the influence of Constantine the Great, for whom the theory was the expression of a fact of personal experience. Constantine's religious policy issues from his unwavering and passionate conviction that he was "the man of God."[27]

We are a long way from the lonely dreams of an Aristides and a Polycarp. To understand how this development in Christianity came to impinge on the Roman world in the way that it did, we must "go backstage" for a moment and look at the precise manner in which the "friend of God" was supposed to have gained his power from its supernatural source.[28]

On one feature, all Late Antique men were agreed. Friendship with the invisible great had the same consequences as friendship with the great of this world: it meant far more than intimacy; it meant power. A good career was one that brought the successful aspirant into face-to-face contact with the powerful: "He lived his first years humbly and in poverty . . . Then he came into friendships and associations and received positions of royal trust . . . He was a friend of kings and governors and became accordingly rich."[29] It was the same with gods: "C'est dans la mesure où l'on a le bonheur d'agréer à un dieu, d'en être aimé, de s'unir plus intimement avec lui, qu'on a la chance aussi de posséder la verité que l'on recherche."[30] This is how Festugière epitomizes the religious experience of the doctor Thessalos. Defeated by failure to discover the occult properties of certain plants, Thessalos went to seek an interview with the god Asclepius. In a dramatic scene of evocation, he can talk face-to-face with the source of medical knowledge. Like the client of the astrologer, he can now be certain of "patronage and success." In his fine exegesis, Festugière stresses the element of revelation in this account: Thessalos has abandoned rational enquiry for reliance on divine authority. This is too modern a criterion. The moral of the story is not that human reason is weak and that the word of a god is strong; but that some men have the luck and the "push" to get access to a divine protector, while others do not: "Oh lucky Thessalos, today a god knows you and soon, when they have heard of your success, men will revere you like a god."[31]

In a society that knew all about the immediate social effects of friendship and patronage, the emergence of men and women who claimed intimate relations with invisible patrons meant far more than the rise of a tender religiosity of personal experience, and more than the groping of lonely men for invisible companionship. It meant that yet another form of "power" was available for the inhabitants of a Mediterranean city.

The problems that Late Antique men faced, therefore, were not whether such power existed, nor whether it rested solely in the Christian church. The power had to be focused and its apparently random distribution canalized trenchantly and convincingly onto a definite class of individuals and a definitive institution. Hence the importance of the rise of the Christian bishop in the third century, and of the Christian holy man in the fourth century.

In the second century, the boundaries between the human and the divine had remained exceptionally fluid. The religious language of the age is the language of an open frontier. Access to divine sources of power was as assiduously informal as access to the person of the emperor in Antonine circles. Hence the importance of the dream in the religious life of the age. It was the paradigm of the open frontier: when a man was asleep and his bodily senses were stilled, the frontier lay wide open between himself and the gods.[32] So we begin our period with prolific dreamers. Through dreams, individuals experienced most clearly and could communicate most cogently the superiority that came from face-to-face contact with the gods. Aelius Aristides had no doubts on this. His dream was "about rhetoric and divine communion": "He said it was fitting that my mind be changed from its present condition, and having been changed, to associate with God, and in association to be superior to man's estate; and neither was remarkable, either by associating with God to be superior, or, being superior, to associate with God."[33] Perpetua and her circle enjoyed a similar sense of superiority: *Tunc dixit mihi frater meus: "Domina soror, iam in magna dignatione es, tanta ut postules visionem et ostenderetur tibi . . ." Et ego quae me sciebam fabulari cum Domino.*[34] It was through her dreams that Perpetua was "on speaking terms with the Lord."

Ease of access, however, meant lack of contour. If divine protection could be as available "as music in an Italian street," then it was open to everybody. There was no reason to believe that the pagan divine man or the Christian martyr enjoyed it on any different terms from the sorcerer or the man in the street, nor that they could wield the power that came from it in any more effective or lasting manner. No unambiguous and permanent "vesting," such as would lodge the divine *dignatio* in specific persons, stood in the

way of continuous and inconclusive competition in spiritual
status. The "friends of God" found themselves competing
in a peer group, in which outright dominance was hard to
achieve. In the late second century, the philosopher was
jostled by the sorcerer, and the Christian bishop by the
Montanist prophetess.

For Christians, the problem was more acute than for
most other groups. In Christian circles direct intimacy
with God was so drastic as to incapacitate the recipient.
Put bluntly, the "power" of the martyr was unambiguous:
but the life expectancy of such a wielder of power was, by
definition, severely limited. We touch on a very savage
streak in the Roman world—exaltation by violence. The
Dream Book of Artemidorus shows that it was not confined
to the Christian imagination. Dreams of the worst experiences of the amphitheater—of being made to fight the wild
beasts,[35] of being burned alive,[36] even of being crucified[37]—
come to be charged with the same frantic imagery of triumph
as that with which the Christian visionaries charged their
own, only too real, sufferings. Poor men liked to dream of
being crucified, for that was to be lifted up.[38] "To be sacri-
ficed at the altar of a god or in public before an assembly of
the people or on the market square brings good luck to
all."[39] It is the death of Polycarp. But to seek vision by death
is the ultimate form of discontinuity. Those who were
insensitive to pain were "already angels";[40] but they
were angels who would soon no longer walk among men.
Martyrdom, however, was only the tip of the iceberg of
Christian attitudes to closeness to the divine. It was a
paradigm of possession. One did not have to be a Montanist,
in the late second century, to believe that the divine was
eminently accessible: "I will pour out my spirit upon all
flesh, and your sons and your daughters shall prophesy,
and your young men shall see visions, and your old men shall

dream dreams."[41] And when this divine was accessible, it could blow through the concrete personality like wind through a broken windowpane.

Possession lay at the heart of the early Christian communities. But it was the kind of possession that emphasized the solidarity and the basically undifferentiated structure of the group. It was benign: in the beautiful language of Irenaeus, it was a bubbling up again from deep inside a man of that blissful unity of feeling that Adam had once known in the morning of creation.[42] The possessed did not stand aside from the group: their skill consisted in making themselves transparent to the values and the needs of the group. The prophets of the *Didaché* were "virtuosi of prayer";[43] the possessed woman known to Tertullian took her material from the readings and the liturgy.[44] Above all, true prophets were men and women who could be observed to surrender all personal initiative. It was the "pseudo-prophet" who kept his wits about him and built up a private practice on the doubts and insecurities of individual members of the community. The true prophet spoke when God caused him to speak and he spoke about the needs of the group as a whole— not about individuals.[45] It is an emphasis on the collective role of prophecy as firm as that of any pagan.

Personal initiative and trance are far from inconsistent, but the degree of personal initiative allowed for the possessed depends very largely on the group that surrounds him. On the whole, what the Christian communities of the second century had wanted was consensus in periods of doubt and conflicting moral standards. This consensus could be precipitated around the opaque figure of the prophet. An element of *bathos*, therefore, attends most prophetic movements of the age.[46] For all his drastic claims, the Paraclete of the Montanists emerged as a fussy and old-fashioned martinet, ministering to the anxieties of small, puritanical groups who felt that they lived on the edge of a very slippery slope. One Christian lady dreamed that an angel had tapped her on the head, remarking that, if she was prepared to leave her pretty head unveiled, why did she not strip all the way down?[47]

At the time of Aelius Aristides, therefore, the Christian "friends of God" were inhibited by a model of access to the divine that was at once too easy and too drastic. The modification of this model in the coming century enabled men like Cyprian to dispense with prophecy, and as bishop of Carthage to stand at the end of an institution with marked, even craggy, contours. It encouraged his successors, two generations later, to face with disturbing equanimity an autocrat who, in thinking of himself as a "man of God," spoke the same language as themselves.

The third-century solution of the problem of contact with the divine came from another strand in the koiné of the Mediterranean. It is usually said that the religious evolution of Late Antiquity is marked by a sharpening of the dichotomy between the self and the body. "That dichotomy comes, of course, from classical Greece—the most far-reaching, and perhaps the most questionable, of all her gifts to human culture."[48]

Yet, for Late Antique people, the more fruitful gift of Greece was the sense of the multiplicity of the self. Plutarch is firm on this: the soul is not simple; it is a composite; and above the many layers of the soul, there lies a true soul that is as superior to it as is the soul to the body.[49] At this peak of the hierarchy of the self Late Antique thinkers placed an invisible and intimate protector, the personal *daimon*, the *genius*, the guardian angel—a powerful invisible being entrusted with the personal care of the individual and conceived of, very largely, as an upward extension of that individual. The outstanding man did not only have a stronger invisible protector. His intimate friendship with that pro-

tector verged on the merging of their identities. In 240 the
young Mani began on his career as a visionary after such
contact with his heavenly Twin: "I made him mine, as my
very own."[50] In 310, Constantine prepared for his conquest
with a vision of *his* Apollo: "You saw him and recognized
yourself in him . . . young and gay, a bringer of salvation
and of exceeding beauty."[51]

The theme of the invisible companion is one of the most
poignant and carefully elaborated strands in Late Antique
religiosity. As Sabine MacCormack has recently written, in
a fine study of the emperor and his *genius* in this period:
"We are dealing with religious consciousness capable of
seeing existence in terms of pairs which could transcend the
boundaries set between the divine and the human spheres."[52]
For Late Antique men, this age-old belief was orchestrated
in such a way as to solve a new problem. It lodged contact
with the divine in the structure of the personality itself.
Great men had great protecting *daimones*; and these protectors were as personal to them as their own souls. Access to
the divine, therefore, was both secure and available to themselves alone. Arthur Darby Nock has said: "A *comes* gave
you the equivalent of a private line."[53] With such permanent
and personal guides, there was less need to seek or to display
spiritual power in the shattering discontinuity of possession
and martyrdom. Furthermore, such a belief defined the
status of a man in this world by connecting him permanently
with a precise stage in the hierarchy of the invisible world.
Observed superiorities did not merely reflect occasional
moments of dramatic face-to-face contact with the divine,
but rather they betrayed an unambiguous and stable relationship with an invisible figure of corresponding rank in
the high-pitched society of heaven.[54] That man of the
world, Ammianus Marcellinus, realized that such a style of
relationship with heaven suited men committed to getting

their own way on earth: "For the theologians maintain that there are associated with all men at their birth . . . certain divinities of that sort, as directors of their conduct; but they have been seen by only a very few, whom their manifold merits have raised to eminence" (*quos multiplices auxere virtutes*).[55]

This theme had always been present in Christian circles; but in the third century it suddenly leaped into focus. Its most passionate exponent was Origen. Here was a man whose warm optimism derived from a sense of being nursed by powerful and loving invisible presences.[56] The Christian going to church enters a building hedged around with guardian angels;[57] his fear of the demonic is allayed by the certainty that angelic presences, also, preside over the weaving of his thoughts;[58] his spiritual progress is a sure ascent of the great sweeping staircase of the angelic hierarchy.

In such a system, the frontier between the divine and the human lies wide open. The upward ceilings of earlier thought have been removed. "The sky's the limit" sums up Origen's view of man. Origen's concept of the "angelic life"—the great hope that men and women might yet live on earth a life according to a higher identity that merged with angelic beings—was a thought that fascinated and repelled Christian ascetics from that time onwards. *Et non erit homo*: it was the highest hope of that age of spiritual ambition.[59]

Yet, with Origen, the high hope had mellowed. It formed part of a continuous process, as the whole visible universe strains to sink even deeper into intimacy with its invisible goal. Even the sun presses against its great resplendent body and sighs: "It would be better if I were dissolved to be with Christ, far better."[60] As a result of this, for all his sharp perfectionism, Origen's view of man was one that placed the main emphasis on the permanent resources of the individual identity and on the slow, sure processes by which this identity unfolded ever higher and higher potentialities. The prophet Daniel, Origen insists, was not "possessed," but he was frequently inspired "by sights and dreams, and at all times he enjoyed the presence of an angel of clear vision."[61] We pass over a watershed in Christian attitudes as to how a man may be formed by his contact with the divine: it is no longer "at once, as once at a crash Paul" but rather, "as Austin, a lingering-out sweet skill."[62]

We can glimpse what such beliefs could mean. In 234, a young man, Gregory, an expatriate from Pontus, the son of a semi-Christian background, had been hanging around the fringes of the imperial bureaucracy at Caesarea in Palestine. He is an example of the many Greeks who flocked to the imperial court after they had learned their Latin and their Roman law at Beirut. It had been a process of acculturation from which Gregory's Greek, according to most scholars, never recovered. In Caesarea, this lonely and disoriented young man came into contact with the study circle of Origen. It was like Augustine coming to Milan: *veni Mediolanum, ad Ambrosium episcopum.*[63]

Gregory found, in the idiom of the guardian angel, a way to make sense of his experience—both of his heady loyalty to Origen and of his own puzzling evolution. In Origen he sensed the presence of the "angel of the great counsel," of Christ himself, just as, at much the same time, Porphyry had learned that Plotinus, his hero, had a god and no mere *daimon* as his protector. For Gregory, belief in his guardian angel was a declaration of faith in a life whose purposes had come to appear all the more firm and its resources all the more rich for being mysteriously discontinuous with the expectations and experiences of the surface of social existence:

Indeed, neither I nor any of my kinsmen could see what was best for me ... For a long time, that angelic presence has nourished me, has formed me and led me by the hand. Above all, he joined me to that great man—to a man who had no previous relationship with me: a man who was no kinsman, no neighbor; who did not come from my province, and had no contact with my home.[64]

At almost the same time, as we now know thanks to the biography of Mani edited by L. Koenen and A. Henrichs, a young man had come to sense his difference from his fellow men in the claustrophobic environment of a sectarian village of southern Mesopotamia. That closed world was being stirred by the last days of Arsacid rule in Seleucia. Western influence, which for Mani took the form of an interest in St. Paul, "that pagan,"[65] trickled in—forerunners of the flood of Christian artisans, builders, silk weavers, and visiting philosophers, who would be drawn to Mesopotamia as the shadow of the Sassanian kings lengthened across the Near East. Like Gregory, Mani thought of himself as having found his own sure course in a wide and confusing world. He made sense of his own experience in similar, if more drastic, imagery. The biography of Mani is the story of a child ringed around with angels. "Coming to me, the spirit [the Heavenly Twin] chose me, judged me fit for him, separated me by drawing me away from the midst of the sect in which I was being reared."[66]

Behind such beliefs, we can sense the pressure of groups that included men like Gregory and who welcomed leaders like Origen and Mani. Let us look at the Christian community of the mid-third century.

We should not think of these communities as missionary groups. If they expanded at all, they did so slowly and erratically. In a society where the family counted for so much, the values of a religion were passed down from parents

to children and spread within the narrow and erratic confines
of the household. The mature convert was a *rara avis.* He
was a swallow who, articulate though he might be, did not
make the summer of an early Christian culture. The mid-
third-century Christian community is most fruitfully imagined as an uneasy conglomeration of Old Christians—for
whom Christianity was an ancestral religion—and a wider
penumbra of half-participants, who, in times of pagan
persecution, were predictable *lapsi,* just as, a century later,
when the Christian church was officially established, they
would be predictable *ficti.* The greatest achievement of such
a group—in discipline, ritual, and literature—was to find a
voice in which to speak to the outside world. This the third-
century church did by means of bishops and teachers, whose
authority came to be vested in the manner I have described
and whose views were often communicated in the intense
teaching situation that Gregory found in the *didaskaleion* of
Origen. Christianity was able to make anyone who found
himself within the Christian community wise after the event.
The Christian teachers offered a view of man and the world
that cut many of the Gordian knots of social living in a
manner that was all the more convincing for being safely
symbolic.

Let us take one example of how the process happened.
In Rome, Justin Martyr was the teacher of uprooted men
from Asia Minor. They already came from Christian families,
but it was his teaching that made sense of their faith.[67]
Any reader of Carl Andresen's *Nomos und Logos* can see how
Justin grappled with the problems posed by their experience
of being "torn away" from their home country and could
have offered them a way of perceiving what had happened
to them. Immigration and the weakening of the bonds of
kinship would not in themselves make a Christian of anyone,[68] but Justin's Christianity, with its emphasis on the

shortcomings of local, regional custom and the superiority of a rational law that could be shared by all men in all situations, would offer the Christian who attended his *didaskaleion* something more than consolation for an abrasive social process.[69] It made the process intelligible, and it allowed the individual to adjust to it, and so to move with it. In this sense, the Christian church could emerge as the unwitting midwife of those very social changes that had weakened the hold of its rivals.

This was the disturbing feature of third-century Christianity. It offered a community which, in symbolic form, clearly accepted the breakdown of the equipoise on which the traditional pagan community had rested. Its initiation was conceived of as producing men shorn of the complexities of their earthly identity. Its ethos produced a more atomistic view of the person, who was less bound than previously to the ties of kinship, of neighborhood, and of region. At the same time, in its attitudes to its leaders, it created in miniature a world that accepted permanent ties of unalloyed loyalty to a high-pitched class of "friends of God."

Christian baptism was a ceremony of simplification: it was not so much a ceremony of rejection and renunciation as of cutting down anomalous and conflicting strands in the life and personality of the baptized.[70] The demonic that was driven out in exorcism was not necessarily conceived of as a persecutory force, standing in enduring hostility to the human race. So dramatic and dualistic an image does not do justice to the nuances of the Late Antique imagination. To a far greater extent, the demons were anomalous creatures.[71] They were incomplete. In Jewish legend they had been those souls for whom God had failed to provide bodies on the evening of the Sabbath.[72] Or they were the result of an undesirable mixing of the categories of heaven and earth. In this latter sense, they were the souls of the offspring of the

mating of the angels with the daughters of men. The baffling
and ambivalent quality of human culture had come from the
secrets revealed—as secrets are revealed on such occasions—
after the momentous lovemaking, by which the boundaries of
heaven and earth had been upset.[73] The skills that brought
tension and confusion on the human community came from
that source: from "the use of antimony and the beautifying
of the eyelids"[74] to "all the blows of death . . . the shield
and the coat of mail and the sword for battle"[75] and "writing
with ink and paper, and thereby many have sinned from all
eternity unto this day."[76] This is an image of the demonic
that made their "earthly power" over the human community
responsible, not only for its obvious misfortunes and mis-
deeds, but also for all the anomaly and confusion that was
latent in human culture and in human social relations.[77] To
the Christians of the second and third centuries, we must
remember, this story of the mating of the angels with the
daughters of men and of its dire consequences for the peace of
society, was not a distant myth: it was a map on which they
plotted the disruptions and tensions around them. When
Tertullian reported the exile of astrologers from Roman
cities, he treated the measure as an attempt to "mop up"
anomalous and disruptive elements which directly continued,
on earth and in his own age, the exile of the fallen angels
from heaven.[78] The Christian therefore stepped from a world
shot through with "loose powers," made dangerous by
incomplete and destructive skills learned from anomalous
sources, into the firm and unambivalent protection of a
guardian angel.[79]

   Under such protection, the power of the stars was no
longer thought to rest upon him.[80] Once again, we must be
precise. The modern scholar expects ancient men to sigh
under the weight of a determinism implied in the astrological
beliefs of the age.[81] A Late Antique man might have faced

his relationships with the stars in a different mood. The influence of the stars was not ineluctable, but baffling. Astrological beliefs condensed an image of man and of his relationship with society that assumed that he lay open to conflicting choices and was subject to a full range of paradoxical triumphs and disasters. Astrology brought down into men's views of their lives and personalities the complexities and conflicts which they saw in the planets as these moved like backgammon counters across the fixity of the heavens.[82] A horoscope was a cobweb of evenly balanced and contradictory forces spun out in the heavens; and a life lived according to a horoscope was a life committed, by men's position in the society in which they lived, to a cat's cradle of profitable and disastrous relationships. The only amusing figure in the solemn procession of fourth-century worthies gathered for us in the *Prosopography of the Later Roman Empire* is the anonymous Roman aristocrat, whose horoscope reveals that mixture of high culture and success in both politics and adultery which the interweaving of the planets offered for such men.[83] An identity formed by the stars, therefore, was a "concourse of opposing powers."[84] So tension-ridden an identity was not for everyone: the conflict and anomaly symbolized by the "revolt and warfare of the [planetary] powers"[85] was a situation that the Christian sought to reduce to order by his baptism. He expected to emerge from it set free, symbolically, from the tensions and anomalies that he saw in himself and in the society around him.

What was emphasized in initiation by this cosmic symbolism, was reiterated in the preaching of the Christian church. A pagan like Celsus might be struck by the way in which Christian demonology was used to "wall off" the Christian group from their fellow men.[86] But we should not be misled by the more radical renunciations encouraged by Christianity

and heroically exemplified by the martyrs. The day-to-day
life of the Christian communities involved less a renunciation
of society as such than a process of symbolic modification and
redirection of its links. This was because the Christian bishop
claimed to be able to answer the question: "Who is my
neighbor?" The third-century answer was more straightforward than was the heroic paradox with which this question
had first been met. Above all, it was reassuringly narrow.
The teaching of the church defined for the Christian who was
not his neighbor: the neighbor of the Christian was *not*
necessarily his kinsman, *not* his fellow dweller in a *quartier*,
not his compatriot or his fellow townsman; his neighbor was
his fellow Christian. It was an answer that became increasingly relevant to the conditions of the Mediterranean towns
of the third century. The model of parity had depended, on
many levels of society, on a tight network of traditional
reciprocities expressed by obligatory gestures. This network
was breaking down and not only among the oligarchies of the
cities. On the humbler level of the "clubbable" life of the
quartier, a monetary inflation made it more difficult to perform
the self-insuring outlays that had cemented the parity of the
group.[87] These pressures placed an increasing strain
on good-neighborliness. Faced by such a situation, the
Christian simply cut the Gordian knot of good-neighborliness, in theory and slowly evolved a system of ideas and
ritual actions that enabled him to create a new form of
neighborliness on his own more straightforward terms. In
imagination, at least, he had dropped some of the ballast of a
tension-ridden society.

   This is best seen at its most intimate—in Christian attitudes to the kin and to the after-life. Dead relatives could
weigh heavily on ancient men. Tertullian mentions the
spirits of dead kinsmen as one of the forces in possession.[88]
When St. Perpetua suddenly uttered the name of her brother

Deinocrates in prayer,[89] she would have been in the grip
of the dead in the same way—of a brother whose death from
a cancer on the cheek had all the horror that surrounds the
"evil death" in a small community.[90] The divine *dignatio*
that rested on Perpetua, however, gave her the power to
see that, as a result of her prayers, Deinocrates had recovered
in the other world the health and innocence of childhood.[91]
Perpetua had come to the brink of a death quite as evil as
that of her brother before she could be freed of his memory.[92]
The average Christian was given less drastic ritual means of
committing the responsibility of the souls of his departed
kin safely to God. In theory at least, God looked after them
in the other world, and not their survivors in this. The rose
crowns of the *Rosalia* were not necessary, a Christian apolo-
gist pointed out, where Christ had crowned the dead with
an eternal garland.[93] Even the *refrigerium* subtly changed
meaning. The living no longer brought to the dead what
their shades lacked; instead they shared around the grave
the peace which they knew the dead now enjoyed securely,
without making further demands on the living.[94] Small
facts show the loosening of the grip of the kin. If we are to
believe Ramsay's evaluation of the Christian tombs of
northern Phrygia, we find that the stubborn privacy of the
family grave opens slowly under Christian influence: out of
seventy-five epitaphs of pagans, only three envisage room
for the body of a friend who is not a member of the family;
out of twenty-six Christian inscriptions, at least seven admit
an outsider.[95] The Christians of the third century loved their
neighbors, but this may have been because they belonged to
a growing body of people who were a little more determined
than in any previous period of ancient history to choose their
neighbors. For a pagan observer, such love would have
confirmed his worst suspicions of the basically egotistical
quality of the age.

Such men chose their leaders. The career and attitudes of
Cyprian shows this clearly. Here is a man who is never alone.
The *clientela* of the urban magnate stuck to him.[96] His
extensive properties mysteriously survived the renunciation
that followed his conversion.[97] Like all great houses, they
had remained a center of relief and a focus of dependence;[98]
their confiscation in itself could be taken as recognition of his
dominant status as bishop of Carthage. Nor could he act
alone. He planned even his death, by skillfully using the
year's delay granted to him in his dream, so as best to suit
the needs of the community he headed. He was determined to
lead. As with any late Roman emperor, his entry into epis-
copal office was held to be the manifestation of a judgment of
God that was merely ratified by men and then shown to men
in the form of the constant protection and inspiration that
surrounded his every stroke of statesmanship.[99] *Dignatio*
rested on his decision making quite as heavily as on the
nature of his death.[100] It is not surprising that, facing a man
whose resolution and diplomatic skills had sunk roots deep
into his dream life, the proconsul pronounced the sentence of
execution *vix et aegre*: Cyprian, the "standardbearer" of
the "criminal confederation" had outmaneuvered him even
to death.[101]

In Cyprian's writings on his church, we see the emergence
of an ideal community where the third-century facts of life are
accepted with unalloyed enthusiasm. It was a high-pitched
community: *dignatio, dignitas,* and, above all, *gloria* raise
some men far above their fellows.[102] Whether he is skillfully
grafting the prestige of the *confessores* into the clerical
oligarchy of Carthage, praising the families of martyrs, or
justifying his own flexible course by reference to dreams and
visions, Cyprian knew how to conjure up in his letters to other
communities the potent mirage of a privileged society.[103]
There was more to this than a mere borrowing of motifs

from the secular world of status and ambition.[104] Cyprian and his church had entered as a competitor into this world. Tertullian may be called *ecclesiarum sophista*; his exuberance and eccentricity reflect a more easy age. Cyprian is panegyrist of the church: a man who can orchestrate those characteristically Late Roman skills we have learned to savor, by which the Late Roman *rhetor* could communicate in acceptable form the outright dominance of one man.

Cyprian was no emperor. He had his critics, who would say, as of Joseph: *Ecce ille somniator venit*.[105] Two generations later, however, the dreamer came: and the dreams of Constantine were unanswerable. Yet Constantine felt at his ease among the Christian bishops. They spoke the same language as himself. Their power was held to be ratified "by the will of God," [106] "given by Heaven" :[107] they, also, had God as their *comes*.[108] Given the spiritual climate of the late third century, the title of "man of God," which Constantine used of himself with the full approval of the leaders of the Christian church, does not sit incongruously on the first Christian emperor.

But Constantine, the "man of God," and his new colleagues were not the only bearers of that title. They were the younger contemporaries of men who had begun to carry the role in society of the "friend of God" yet one stage further. In Egypt, Anthony, the "man of God" had passed through the early trials of his ascetic life before Constantine fought the battle of the Milvian Bridge in 312; Pachomius had founded his first community at Tabennisi a few years before Constantine gained control of the eastern provinces of the Roman Empire in 324. In the making of Late Antiquity, the monks of Egypt played a role more enduring than that of Constantine.

4

FROM THE HEAVENS
TO THE DESERT:
ANTHONY AND PACHOMIUS

Those who came to Egypt in the fourth century came to a
foreign country, with many surprises: "Once we arrived
from Syria to Abba Poimen, to ask him about hardness of
heart. The old man knew no Greek nor was there any
interpreter present. Seeing us in a quandary, Poimen
(unpredictable as ever) began as best he could to speak
Greek."[1]

The social and religious history of Late Roman Egypt
has suffered from being treated in isolation. Heavy emphasis
has been placed on what Egypt did *not* share with the
remainder of the Mediterranean world. A view of Egypt as
a region whose population is held to have been locked away
in varying degrees from the rest of the Roman world rests
heavily on our interpretation of the ascetic movement. It
has made it exceptionally difficult to assess the relevance of
the experiences of the monks of fourth-century Egypt to the
Mediterranean-wide "debate of the holy," which entered a
crucial phase in the age of Constantine, Anthony, and Pachomius. Yet, like the art and architecture of Coptic Egypt, the
exuberant growth of the ascetic movement was not the
product of a monolithic and encapsulated "national" tradi-

tion. It was an exceptionally skillful and consequential working through, in distinctive local conditions, of the themes of a Mediterranean-wide *koiné*.[2] This consideration goes some way to explain the role of Egypt in the Mediterranean world of the fourth century. Egypt became "a splendid theater" in which the basic themes developed in the Christian communities of the third century came to be acted out with inimitable clarity and gusto before an audience drawn from all classes and regions of the Roman world. I wish to draw attention, therefore, to this particular aspect of the lives of Anthony, Pachomius, and their successors. The literature of the ascetic movement enables us to pass under a microscope some of the themes that had risen to prominence in the course of the third century. We can take these themes out of the crowded and confused life of the Christian communities in town and village, and, with the hermits, watch them blossom into new, largely unexpected growths, in the clear light of the desert.

For, if we turn to the Egyptian villages of the late third or early fourth centuries, we can trace a further, and more radical, ramification of the Christian response to the breakdown of the old solidarities. The overwhelming impression given by the literature of the early Egyptian ascetics, is that we are dealing with men who found themselves driven into the desert by a crisis in human relations. They came to analyze the tensions among their fellow men with anxious attention. They spoke about these with an authority and an insight that make *The Sayings of the Desert Fathers*[3] the last and one of the greatest products of the Wisdom Literature of the ancient Near East. Ascetic literature points backwards to a milieu where the tensions of living in the "world" had proved unbearable. Deep in the desert, monks still spoke to each other of the crowded life of the Nile Valley: "How is the world? And does the Water [the Nile] come

at the right time?"[4] The very existence of the monks spoke
to the village about itself and its values, just as, most poignantly, the village still spoke to them:

> A brother once lived outside his village, and for many years
> he did not go there, and he said to the brethren: "Look how
> many years I have been here, and have not gone over to my
> village; and you, look how often you have been there." They
> told Abba Poimen about him, and the old man said: "By night
> I used to go out and walk right round the fields of my village,
> lest my heart glory that I had never been back to my village.[5]

From sources such as *The Sayings of the Desert Fathers*,
therefore, we can hope to obtain a negative from which
to make a print of the "friction points" of an Egyptian
village at the time of the ascetic movement.

The villages appear to have been passing through a crisis
of solidarity more acute than the usual unresolved tensions of
peasant life. The tension was as old as the village itself. A
village was a sumtotal of separate households. Autarky and
total disengagement from the restraints of their neighbors
were ideals which, though never realized, molded the hopes
of Egyptian farmers. Neighborliness was always under strain.
In Palestine, "The villagers say that the prophet Mohammed
ordered the good treatment of neighbors as far as the seventh
house from one's own."[6] The evidence of Late Roman Egypt
shows that the Prophet was optimistic. The villages from
which the ascetics came were not inhabited by the docile
and overtaxed *fellahin* of modern imagination, but by
singularly abrasive small farmers, for whom violence of
body and tongue alike were normal:[7] "'He who dwells
with breathren' said Abba Matoes 'must be not square, but
round, so as to turn himself toward all.' He went on: 'It is
not through virtue that I live in solitude, but through
weakness; those who live in the midst of men are the strong
ones.'"[8] Yet detachment was out of the question. For

economic insecurity, the demands of taxation and the ineluctable discipline of the Water, the need to cooperate in order to control the precious water of the Nile, forced households of natural egotists into constant, humiliating, and friction-laden contact and collaboration with their fellows.

Tensions such as these were the stuff of peasant life; but in the late third century they became more acute because their poles were more distinct, and the resolution that some members of the village achieved was all the more radical for having found an explicit religious vehicle. In the first place, the possibility of individual advancement, at the level of the village landowner, became greater than it had been in previous generations. In the fourth century, Egyptian villagers emerge as peasant-proprietors.[9] Many peasants had been only too successful in rising above their fellows. At a time when the average holding in some villages was forty-four *arourae*,[10] the family of St. Anthony owned some three hundred, "very fertile and beautiful to see."[11] In the house of Abba Theodore, there was enough food even in mid-winter; and he began his career in a cell he had built in his own well-kept garden.[12] Throughout Late Antiquity, the study of recruitment to the ascetic movement and of the endowment of the great monasteries takes us away from the better-known categories of Late Roman social life, from the great landowner and the dependant peasant to the more ambiguous, but no less influential, class of the "comfortable farmer."

At exactly the same period, however, when farmers might have expected to make their own way, unrestrained by their neighbors, they found themselves thrown back upon each other by the increased weight of taxation, which rested on the village as a whole. Thus, in the generation when the individual might have hoped to "go it alone" more successfully than ever before, the tensions and frictions of communal living reasserted themselves in a particularly abrasive manner. Disengagement, *anachōrēsis*, was the reflex reaction of Egyptian farmers in a difficult position. It was possible to move to another village[13] or to seek some similar way of disentangling oneself from one's fellows. We meet such a farmer in the person of Aurelius Isidore. Here was a "comfortable farmer" of the new style: illiterate, yet possessing a handsome collection of legal documents and complaints in his own interest, Isidore's holdings had increased by some ninety *arourae* between 299 and 310. Throughout his career, he weathered the storms of village life by a canny insistence on noninvolvement. He was, he insisted, "a man of modest means." When his house was attacked in 316 he knew exactly how to present himself: "Although I possess a good deal of land and am occupied with its cultivation, I am not involved with any person in the village but keep to myself" (*kata emauton anachōrountos*).[14]

Isidore's *anachōrēsis* was a politic withdrawal. Yet it shows how close to the surface of men's minds the ideal of noninvolvement lay. In the cites, Christianity had already evolved a language of disengagement. It was in a Christian church that Anthony found an answer to the thoughts which had already begun to trouble him: "He chanced to be on his way to church. As he was walking along, he collected his thoughts and reflected how the Apostles left everything and followed the Savior."[15]

Hence the enduring appeal of the holy man of ascetic origin to the peasant societies of the Late Antique Mediterranean. In his act of *anachōrēsis* he had summed up the logical resolution of a dilemma with which the average farmer, and more especially the average successful farmer, could identify himself wholeheartedly:

Sometimes you hear, fifth-hand,
As epitaph:
He chucked up everything
And just cleared off.
And always the voice will sound
Certain you approve
This audacious, purifying
Elemental move.[16]

For the act of *anachōrēsis* in itself, rather than any exceptional supernatural powers, was what the audience of the hermit saw in him. His powers and his prestige came from acting out, heroically, before a society enmeshed in oppressive obligations and abrasive relationships, the role of the utterly self-dependent, autarkic man.[17]

It is here that third-century themes take on a new, more radical meaning in the minds of fourth-century monks. The monk was the "lonely man" par excellence. His decision to "sit alone" in the desert gave reality to a long tradition of speculation on the lost simplicity of Adam: the "glory of Adam" was summed up in his person.[18] Yet the drastic quality of the ascetic renunciation accounts for a crucial difference between third-century theory and fourth-century practice. The *anachōrēsis* of the fourth-century hermit took place in a world that was exceptionally sensitive to its *social* meaning. It was a gesture that had originated in tensions between man and man; and the ascetic message derived its cogency from having resolved those tensions.

For this reason, the Desert Fathers lavished the most meticulous attention on those links that bound men, disastrously, to other men, and not on the links that bound men's souls to their bodies. Alongside a "vertical" imagery by which the soul demonstrated its closeness to a "heavenly" source of power by brutal triumph over the "earthly" region of the body, we find equal prominence given to a forceful "horizontal" imagery.[19] Even in his most personal

and private acts of mortification, as when he triumphed over
the needs of his own sexuality, the ascetic was seen as
acting out a dramatic and readily intelligible ritual of social
disengagement. As a result, "heavenly" power on earth
came to be associated less with an intangible relationship to
the other world and more with a clear ascetic stance to this
world. A relationship to heaven was shown most irrefutably
by a move to the desert.

A look at the temptations of the ascetics will make this
plain. Let us begin with the obvious: what did they make of
the "demon of fornication"? Not quite what we would have
made of it. There is no doubt that our own experiences of
sexuality and that of the early hermits overlapped at some
points: "The devil changed himself into an Ethiopian maiden
whom I had once seen in my youth in the summertime picking
reeds, and came and sat on my knee."[20] But if we go on to
ask what was the precise meaning of sexuality in the overall
life of such men, then we get an answer that is both less
modern and more serious. The woman stood for all that was
most stable and enveloping in the life of men. When a man
dreams of his wife, Artemidorus wrote, he is usually thinking
of his job: "The woman stands either for the profession
of the dreamer or for his business obligations."[21]

When a hermit was attacked by the "demon of fornication," therefore, his thoughts were straying not so much to
the sexual needs of his body as to the dire constraints of the
village:

Abba Olympios of the Cells was tempted to fornication. His
thoughts said to him, "Go, and take a wife." He got up,
found some mud, made a woman and said to himself, "There
is your wife, now you must work hard in order to feed her."
So he worked giving himself a great deal of trouble. The next
day, making some mud again, he formed it into a girl and
said to his thoughts, "Your wife has had a child, you must work

harder so as to be able to feed her and clothe your child."
So he wore himself out doing this, and said to his thoughts,
"I cannot bear this weariness any longer." They answered,
"If you cannot bear such weariness, stop wanting a wife."
God, seeing his efforts, took away the conflict from him and
he was at peace.[22]

By contrast, anger, a sin of human relations, bulked
larger with the ascetics than did the "demon of fornication,"
which lurked in their bodies. In addition to sexual temptation, anger and the evils of speech were the stuff of village
life: "A brother asked him [Abba Isidore], 'Why are the
demons so frightened of you? The old man said to him,
Because I have practised asceticism since the day I became a
monk and not allowed anger to reach my lips.'"[23] Abba
Isidore said, "One day I went to the marketplace to sell
some small goods; when I saw anger approaching me, I left
the things and fled."[24] Abba Agatho went for three years
with a stone in his mouth so that he should learn silence.[25]
The most poignant anecdotes in monastic literature are about
the use of words:

> An old man who came to Abba Achilles found him spitting
> blood out of his mouth. He asked him "What is the matter,
> Father?" The old man answered, "The word of a brother
> grieved me. I struggled not to tell him so and I prayed God
> to rid me of this word. So it became like blood in my mouth
> and I have spat it out. Now I am in peace, having forgotten the
> matter."[26]

The ascetic was a man who had made himself "dead."
But the death was a social death and not the mortification of
the body. By cutting away all dependence on his fellows, the
ascetic had gained the *insouciance* of the grave.[27] And this is
how the archaeologist has found their cells in the desert at
Esna: they had lived in these, "comme ensevelis vivants dans
une retraite qui pourrait être une tombe: mais ils ne recher-
chent pas l'épreuve physique, la privation, la douleur."[28]

The total disengagement and social "death" implied
in the gesture of *anachōrēsis* left the ascetics shorn of the
normal social supports of identity. The hermit was regarded
as a man who had set about finding his true self. By the fact
of *anachōrēsis* he had resolved the tensions and incoherences
of his relations with his fellow men. In the desert, he was
expected to settle down, in conflict with the demonic, to
resolve the incoherences of his own soul. The powers the
ascetic wielded came from a long process of self-discovery.
Paul the Simple served Anthony in the desert for many years.
After he had performed his due quota of acts of obedience,
the old man said to him: "Now you have become a monk;
remain alone in order that you may be tried by demons. So
Paul dwelt there one year and was counted worthy of grace
over demons and diseases." [29]

In entering into the experiences of an Anthony and a Paul,
and in reconstructing what such experiences meant to
contemporaries, we should not be misled by the long tradition of the iconography of the Temptation of Saint Anthony.[30]
The concern of the hermit was more down to earth and less
melodramatic. Anthony was grappling with his own personality. He did so in a situation of self-imposed sensory
deprivation, where one may suspect that hallucination and
extreme emotional states were deliberately courted so as to be
overcome and not entered into unwittingly and then naively
ascribed to the demonic. The ascetic preoccupation with the
demonic was merely the shadow side of the third-century
emphasis on the protecting spirit as an upward extension
of the self.[31] The hermit's personality, as thus mapped out
for him by the religious *koiné* of the age, wavered between
the stable guardianship of Christ[32] and of his protecting
angel[33] and the unstable, incoherent forces of the demonic.
The language used of Anthony's experiences draws its
clarity and its cogency from speaking of the demonic in

terms of forces external to the self. As A. D. Nock has said of the mysteries (and Anthony was thought of as having emerged from his ordeal "as one initiated into sacred mysteries") :[34] "It was a way of expressing mystical or prophetic intuitions which came to a man as though from without, so that he seemed to himself to be acted upon rather than acting." [35]

Yet we should be careful not to miss the nuance by which, like the guardian angel, the demonic was sensed as an extension of the self. A relationship with the demons involved something more intimate than attack from outside: to "be tried by demons" meant passing through a stage in the growth of awareness of the lower frontiers of the personality. The demonic stood not merely for all that was hostile *to* man; the demons summed up all that was anomalous and incomplete *in* man.[36] Demons, incomplete creatures, sought completion through human complicity: "Abraham, the disciple of Abba Agatho, questioned Abba Poemen saying: 'How do the demons fight against me?' Abba Poemen said to him: 'The demons fight against you? . . . Our own wills become the demons, and it is these which attack us in order that we may fulfil them.'" [37] To understand and to reject the demonic was an act of self-exorcism analogous to the symbolic achievement of "simplicity" through the exorcism of baptism. It closed disturbingly open frontiers in the self.[38] Hence, for all the many accounts of confrontations of ascetics with the demonic, few spiritual traditions have placed such a ferocious emphasis on self-awareness. Self-awareness and awareness of the demonic form a pair. In the *Sayings of the Fathers*, Egyptian hermits appear far more preoccupied with their trains of thought, their *logismoi*, than with the demonic that lurked behind them: "It was said of Abba Poimen that every time he prepared to go to the *Synaxis*, he sat alone and examined his thoughts for about an hour and then he set off." [39] "He who does not reveal his thoughts causes them to rise up against him, and he who says his thoughts with confidence before the Fathers chases them away in peace and quiet." [40]

A dogged concern with creating a new identity by social death and by prolonged introspection meant that the relationship with the supernatural that was most prized in ascetic circles differed, in significant ways, from the type of relationship that contemporary Egyptian pagans expected to enjoy. The monks of Egypt mark a turning of the ways. We must look at them for a moment against the background of the Late Antique paganism from which so many, Pachomius among them, had come, and of which we frequently catch glimpses, in the person of traveling priests,[41] of curious philosophers,[42] and in the silent presence of the deserted temples in which so many came to sit.[43]

What we had found in the "style" of the religious life of that late second and third centuries was that the frontier between the divine and the human had lain tantalizingly open. The "friend of God" expected to tap an ever available reservoir of power and blessing. The contact with the divine that summed up this "style" most effectively was the most informal, the dream vision,[44] but the more drastic methods of possession and of evocation also emphasized the closeness of the supernatural by stressing the permeability to it of human flesh and the efficacy of human ritual in entering into immediate contact with it.

The pagan religiosity of Late Antique Egypt appears to have opted heavily for that particular style of access to the divine. The pagan prophet was still a force to be reckoned with in the third century.[45] The *Oracle of the Potter*, which had come to a priest when in trance, still circulated in the fourth century.[46] Paganism did not "wither away" in Egypt. It is misleading to suppose that a split between the isolated and

uprooted paganism of a Hellenized minority and a resurgent
Coptic-speaking "national" Christianity aided the growth of
Christian asceticism. Like its Coptic art, Egypt in the fourth
and fifth centuries remained equally divided between Christian
and pagan elements. We are dealing with a tenacious sub-
classical paganism of Greek idiom but with deep local roots.
The Dionysos and the Hermes of Coptic carving and textiles
might not have impressed Pheidias, but it was in this almost
fairy-tale guise that the old gods had remained forces to be
reckoned with in the towns and villages of Egypt.[47]

By the beginning of the fourth century, a silent religious
war was being waged in the villages of Egypt.[48] The issues
of the conflict were made plain in terms of the availability of
the supernatural. For the pagan, the gods still lay close to
hand. Their blessing was part of the weave of the normal
social life of a settled community: they were there when the
priests called them. "One of the Old Men of the Thebaid
said, 'I was the son of a pagan priest. When I was young, I
used to sit and watch my father frequently going in to perform sacrifices to his idol. Once, sneaking in behind him, I saw
Satan and all his host standing in a vision before him.'"[49]

Pachomius and the monks of the Thebaid came directly
from pagan backgrounds. They fought their own past, and
they did so by creating a new style of religious life, that was
the antithesis of that against which they had rebelled. On the
issue of easy access to the divine, they made *il gran rifiuto*.
They brought down a sense of their own identity, defined by
its sinful thoughts and urgings, like a "wall of darkness"[50]
between themselves and the shimmering, tantalizing presences of the other world.

The easy-going intimacy of an earlier age vanished:

> The nearer a man draws to God, the more he sees himself a
> sinner. It was when Isaiah the prophet saw God, that he
> declared himself "a man of unclean lips."[51]

How is it that some can say, "We see visions of the angels?"
The Old Man said: "Happier by far is he who can see his own
sins at all times."[52]

Abba Olympios said this: "One of the pagan priests came
down from Scetis one day and came to my cell and slept there.
Having reflected on the monks' way of life, he said to me,
'Since you live like this, do you receive any visions from your
god?' I said to him, 'No.' Then the priest said to me, 'Yet,
when we make a sacrifice to our god, he hides nothing from us,
but discloses his mysteries: and you, giving yourselves so
much hardship, vigils, prayers and asceticism, say that you
see nothing?'"[53]

The stance of the monks was a crushing rebuke to the
religious style of the pagan world. A studied rejection of the
usual manner of wielding power in society from supernatural
sources completed the process of *anachōrēsis*. The monks
sidestepped the ambivalences involved in claims to exercise
"heavenly" power in "earthly" regions. They defined
"heavenly" power quite simply as power that was not to be
used: "Some say of Abba Anthony that he became a bearer
of the Holy Spirit, but he did not wish to speak of this
because of men, for he could see all that passed in this world
and could tell all that would come to pass."[54]

There was, of course, an element of *panache* in so studious
a rejection of supernatural power.[55] It was a case of *reculer
pour mieux sauter*: the monks gained more power through
rejecting it. In Egypt, and in other parts of the Mediterranean world, they brought about the emergence of the holy
man in his definitive Late Antique form. This involved the
lodging of spiritual power in individuals in an ever firmer
manner, and the application of this power, in the monastic
movement, to the creation of permanent institutions.
The holy man in Egypt marks the culmination of the process
begun among the leaders of the Christian urban community
in the third century: supernatural power did not only exist,

it had to be seen to exist, securely vested in an observable and continuous manner in certain human beings and in no others. This the ascetic could offer. His power did not come from discontinuous moments of trance, vision, or dream. Nor could it be gained by means available to the average man, by dreams or by the observance of traditional rituals. Instead, an utterly distinctive lifestyle, clearly delineated from the moment of his first move from the settled community to the desert and doggedly maintained for decades, was what was held to have gained him the powers that he wielded. The holy man had to work and to be seen to work. Charisma was the visible manifestation of an equally visible ascetic "labor," whose rhythms and physical effect were palpable to all.[56]

Furthermore, *anachōrēsis* placed supernatural power beyond the ambiguities of the "earthly" regions by having grown it, in pure culture as it were, in the antithesis to human society. Prolonged rituals of social disengagement reassured the clientele of the ascetic that his powers were totally acceptable, because they were wielded by a man dead to human motivation and dead to human society.

Behind the growing status of the ascetic in the Christian community as a whole there was the conviction that whereas the pagan priest might gain his power with ease, even with elation, from traditions handed to him by the settled community, the monk brought to his task the weight of a lifetime spent outside human society, in states of prolonged depression and anxious self-searching.[57] The sharp taste of individual suffering had given him the power of vision.

> His eyes are quickened so with grief,
> He can watch a grass or leaf
> Every instant grow. He can
> Clearly through a flint wall see,
> Or watch the startled spirit flee,
> From the throat of a dead man.[58]

Gained, in this manner, by personal experience, the power of vision was applied, first and foremost, to the "searching of hearts." Thus, while the pagan "friend of the gods" might peer into the other world, the fourth-century Christian holy man was valued because he could turn his gaze back toward his fellow humans. The first monastic leaders completed an evolution begun by the bishops of the third century. Groups formed by a crisis of human relations needed to invest their leaders with a supernatural ability to handle these.[59] In the increasingly unmanageable Christian communities of the third century, the wish to be certain of oneself and of one's fellows had been poignantly felt:

> Next we arrived at a very bright spot, and our garments began to glow, and our bodies became even more brilliant than our bright clothing. Indeed, our flesh became so bright that one's eyes could see the secrets of the heart. Then, looking into my own bosom, I saw some stains . . . And Lucian came up to me . . . and I said to him, "Those stains, you know, are there because I did not at once make up with Julianus."[60]

The idea that God could search the heart was central to the Christian sensibility of the age. Cyprian never tired of citing *Homo videt in faciem, Deus in cor* (1 Sam. 16: 7).[61] "I know this through many examples, but I can measure it by my own experience. There were in me, first, things which fell short of righteousness. Nor did I think that there was any celestial power who could see into the recesses of my heart. But Almighty God, seated in the watchtower of heaven . . ."[62] These are the words of a typical Christian convert of the age—Constantine. The greatest gift that God might give to men placed in a special relationship with Him was the gift of His all-seeing eye to peer into the hearts of men:[63] "Come to me, come, I say, to the *man of God*. Believe that by my questions the secret places of your heart will be searched out by me."[64] These are the words of a typical Christian leader—Constantine again.

It is in this context that we meet the great Pachomius. Pachomius and his successor Theodore were held to have been able to achieve, in the exemplary conditions of a great monastery, what the bishops and the other religious leaders of the third century had failed to achieve. They had founded and maintained an institution on a gift to search hearts. It was this gift that concerned the bishops who examined Pachomius: "We confess that you are a man of God, and we know that you can see the demons . . . But on the issue of the searching of hearts, as this is a great matter, tell us more of that, that we may persuade those who complain against you."[65]

The gift, *to dioratikon*, was held to be the secret of Pachomius' ability to organize and to control a landslide of conversions to the ascetic life in Upper Egypt. He was the kind of leader the monks needed: the identity of each one was transparent to him. The great Pachomian monasteries were vast, impersonal places. Even at the base of the trees, fallen fruit would be lined up in neat rows, to be collected only by duly appointed officers.[66] Over two thousand monks might come together, squatting on the ground at a great festival. Yet Abba Theodore would go round that crowd, stepping from one monk to another, and telling to each what each had on his mind.[67]

In the same way, in the clarity of the desert, a great ascetic like Abba Macarius could step into the place of the all-seeing father figure left vacant, through the sheer unmanageability of urban conditions, by the bishops of his age. Like the bishop of the *Apostolic Constitutions*, Macarius was an *epigeios theos*: "They said of Abba Macarius the Great that he became, as it is written, a god upon earth because, just as God protects the world, so Abba Macarius would cover the faults which he saw."[68] *Epigeios theos*: the term sums up the Late Antique revolution. Heaven and earth have come to be joined in the figure of a human being, and this joining has been brought about so that other human beings could enter the life of a newly formed group under his guidance. "Heavenly" power is used, on earth, by human beings to rule other human beings.[69] I would agree with a biographer of Pachomius: "True indeed is the oft-repeated proverb: 'Egypt does not give birth to many; but when she does, it is a great one.'"[70]

Two generations only separate the outstanding career of Cyprian from the reign of Constantine and the *anachōrēsis* of Anthony and Pachomius. In this short time, a long "debate on the holy" was brought to a close. The outlines of the situation that characterized Late Antiquity had emerged. A special class of men had come to wield growing power in Roman society by reason of their exceptional relationship with the supernatural. On all levels of its experience, Late Antique society was alert to the exceptional and prepared to acclaim it. Men had come to accept and to give clear expression to the facts of power and hierarchy in the world around them. As a result, the resources of a whole culture, legislation, ceremonials, literature, art, and architecture, converged to highlight the status of a new spiritual elite of "friends of God."

Yet the growing clarity that becomes so marked a feature of the late third and fourth centuries was gained at a heavy cost. A wide range of alternatives came to be closed. This closing of alternatives is only indirectly associated with the rise of Christianity and the decline of paganism. Instead, we sense that the *koiné* of Mediterranean religious experience as a whole has shifted in an insensible tide that washed all its shores and has touched all its inhabitants. Pagans and Christians alike took up a new stance to another "style" of religious life, in which expectations of what human beings could achieve in relation to the supernatural had changed subtly and irreversibly from the age of the Antonines. The change cut off the Christian church quite as much from its own past as from its pagan contemporaries. A new form of Christian religiosity ratified the new position of Christian leaders in Roman society.

We are dealing, in the fourth century, with a sensibility that was at once more somber and yet more stable in its expectations of where the *locus* of the supernatural was to be found. The Christian bishop, the Christian "holy man," the physical remains of the Christian martyr stand out all the more clearly because the upward ceiling of human contact with the divine has come to be drawn more firmly. For the Christians of the fourth and fifth centuries, the power that came from contact with the supernatural was not for everyone to use. Even for those who might enjoy it, such contact was considered to be fraught with crushing hardship. The prolonged "labors" and the crushing sense of sin that characterized the ascetic life condensed, in the persons of the new ascetic heroes, the privileges and the heavy burdens of an exceptional class of human beings.

Some Christian theological controversies of the late fourth and early fifth centuries show how the tide had turned. The tranquil ease of access to the supernatural that had given such confidence to Origen and that underlay his heady perfectionism now seemed to belong to a distant, more turbulent age of equal spiritual opportunities. The perfectionism latent in Origen's teaching, and its Western equivalent, the teaching of Pelagius, were both condemned within a generation by bishops and clergymen, all of whom had, in various ways, been tinged by the new flavor of ascetic sensibility. Augustine sat down to write the melancholy tenth book of the *Confessions*, to prove by relentless introspection that "surely all life on earth is a temptation," at the same moment as Abba Poimen passed on the saying of Anthony: "The greatest thing that a man can do is to throw

his faults before the Lord and to expect temptation to his
last breath."[71] In the Christian church, the spiritual dominance of the few was made ever firmer and more explicit
by a denial of ease of access to the supernatural that would
have put "heavenly" power in the hands of the average
sinful believer.

Pagans watched this development with deep religious
anger. For in the "debate on the holy" Late Antique pagan
sentiment maintained to the last one feature of the traditional
position: the supernatural was constantly available to men.
From the refined Proclus to the Egyptian priest of a village
shrine, pagans continued to be comforted by the ancient
belief that heaven and earth lived side by side in gentle
communion. To deny this was the supreme blasphemy.[72]
To a pagan, those rites that had been handed down since the
beginnings of the human race and that had been preserved
in the settled and continuous society crowded around the
Mediterranean enabled human beings, without doing
violence to their normal relations with their fellows, to
draw quietly upon an ever present reservoir of power,
blessing, and inspiration. As Ammianus Marcellinus wrote:
"The elemental powers, when propitiated by diverse rites,
supply mortals with prophecy, as if from the veins of in-
exhaustible founts."[73] For such men, the easy-going unity
of heaven and earth somehow mirrored the unity and
solidarity of the civilization they had inherited, which had
passed on to them such a richness of well-tried means of
access to the other world.

Among the pagans, therefore, the crisis of a great tradition
was sensed as nothing less than a crisis in the relations of
heaven and earth. A striking new exegesis of the iconography of a *mithraeum* has made the issue plain: "The central
claim of the mysteries to authority and legitimacy rested
precisely upon this complex of correspondences with the

nature and order of the cosmos."[74] The pagan still expected to feel embedded in this cosmos. The Christians had brutally torn the network of correspondences on which pagan belief depended. Hence the anger with which Plotinus rounded on those Christian-influenced "Gnostics," who refused to be either humbled or consoled by the majesty of the cosmos:

> Yet imbeciles are found to accept such teaching at the mere sound of the words "You yourself are to be nobler than all else, nobler than men, nobler than even gods." Human audacity is very great. A man once modest, restrained and simple hears, "You, youself, are the child of God; those men whom you used to venerate, those beings whose worship they inherit from antiquity, none of these are His children; you without lifting hand are nobler than the very heavens."[75]

The Christians looked to the earth alone. They claimed power from heaven; but they had made that heaven remote and they kept its power to themselves, to build up new separate institutions among upstart heroes on earth. Such institutions had been hastily thrown up by men for men. To these human institutions a new generation of Christians was prepared to transfer that sense of solemn delight which men of the old religion still sought in the clustering stars. The "stars" that held the attention of a fourth-century Christian were the tombs of the martyrs, scattered like the Milky Way throughout the Mediterranean.[76] The lives of human heroes, the spiritual struggles of the individual, and the fate of traditions of doctrine passed from one human intermediary to the other in highly self-conscious, inward-looking institutions, came to hold the attention of men to the exclusion of those old problems whose solution had lain in placing man correctly against the overwhelming backdrop of the cosmos.[77]

When Iamblichus took issue with Porphyry, writing as Abammon the Egyptian prophet, his words were, indeed, prophetic. The austere philosophical transcendentalism of

Porphyry threatened to deny that the gods were available on earth and hence to deny that heaven was accessible to men through the traditional rituals:

> This doctrine spells the ruin of all holy ritual and all communion between gods and men achieved by our rites, by placing the physical presence of the superior beings outside this earth. For it amounts to saying: the divine is at a distance from the earth and cannot mingle with men; this lower region is a desert, without gods. As a result, we priests have been able to learn nothing from communing with the gods; and why should you ask us questions, as if we were any different from other men?[78]

Yet Iamblichus was wrong in one point. The final blow came, not from the philosophical scruples of Porphyry, but from the *anachōrēsis* of the monks of Egypt. The new heroes and leaders of the Christian church came to stand between heaven and an earth emptied of the gods.

The Christian answer to the pagans has been made plain, in part, by the manner in which the "debate on the holy" had unfolded since the age of the Antonines. Throughout that debate, we meet men and women who held doggedly to an obscure intuition, with which they grappled in a language top-heavy with the presence of the supernatural: in a poignant search for some oasis of unalloyed relationships between themselves, they made plain that what human beings had marred only human beings could put right.

NOTES

INDEX

NOTES

1 A DEBATE ON THE HOLY

1. Gregory of Tours, *Passio Septem Dormientium*, 7, *Monumenta Germaniae Historica: Script. rer. Merov.* I, ii (Hanover, 1885), 401.

2. W. H. C. Frend, *Martyrdom and Persecution in the Early Church* (Oxford, 1965), p. 389.

3. See, for example, Peter Brown, "Approaches to the Religious Crisis of the Third Century A.D., " *English Historical Review* 83 (1968), 542–558 = *Religion and Society in the Age of Saint Augustine* (London, 1972), pp. 74–93; Ramsay MacMullen, *Roman Government's Response to Crisis, A.D. 235–337* (New Haven, 1976).

4. E. R. Dodds, *Pagan and Christian in an Age of Anxiety* (Cambridge, 1965), p. 137.

5. A. J. Festugière, *Hermétisme et mystique païenne* (Paris, 1967), p. 70.

6. R. Duncan-Jones, *The Economy of the Roman Empire: Quantitative Studies* (Cambridge, 1974), pp. 259–287. For a firm sense of the limitations of Late Roman urban life, we now have the masterly study of Evelyne Patlagean, *Pauvreté économique et pauvreté sociale à Byzance: 4e–7e siècles* (Paris, 1977), pp. 156–170.

7. Iris Origo, *The Merchant of Prato* (Harmondsworth, 1963), p. 58.

8. Tertullian, *Ad martyras* vi, 1.

9. Arnobius, *Adv. Gentes* I, 1–2: *Ipsos etiam caelites, derelictis curis solemnibus, quibus quondam solebant invisere res nostras, terrarum ab regionibus exterminatos.* Cf. Symmachus, *Relatio* iii, 16: *sacrilegio annus exaruit.* Christian attitudes: Theodosius II, *Novella* iii, 75 (447): *An diutius perferemus mutari temporum vices irata caeli temperie, quae*

paganorum exacerbata perfidia nescit naturae libramenta servare. Sin positively "pollutes" the atmosphere: Ps.-Clement, *Recognitiones* V, 27, 1: *Fatigata sceleribus impiorum vincuntur elementa, et inde est quod aut terrae fructus corrumpitur.* The Liturgy of St. John Chrysostom prays: Ὑπὲρ εὐκρασίας ἀέρων.

10. Eusebius, *Hist. Eccl.* IX, viii, 10. The best comment on this is the late third-century Boglio stele from Siliana in North Africa, where the image of the God and a scene showing the performance of sacrifices is placed above a procession of cars returning loaded from the harvest: R. Bianchi-Bandinelli, *Rome: The Late Empire* (London, 1961), pl. 200 at p. 217.

11. Tertullian, *De pallio* i

12. Ramsay MacMullen, *Roman Social Relations* (New Haven, 1974), pp. 63–69.

13. Ibid., pp. 75–77; L. Cracco-Ruggini, "Le associazioni professionali nel mondo romano-bizantino," *Settimane di Studi sull'Alto Medio Evo* 18.1 (Spoleto, 1971), 79–91.

14. T. D. Barnes, *Tertullian* (Oxford, 1971), pp. 87–88. Christians were exposed to mob violence when they did not participate in pagan festivals: *Apost. Const.* II, 18.

15. Galen, *De praenotione* 4, ed. G. Kühn (Leipzig, 1827), XIV, 624.

16. For a recent egregious example see Peter Hermann, "Ehrendekret von Iulios Gordos," *Anz. österr. Akad. Wiss.* 3 (1974), 439–444. On the stability of such normative values: L. Robert, *Hellenica* 13 (1965), 226–227. See a later Christian inscription in E. Diehl, *Inscriptiones Latinae Christianae Veteres* I (Berlin, 1925), no. 2157: *queius fidelitatem et castitate et bonitate omnes vicinales experti sunt.*

17. E. R. Dodds, *Pagan and Christian,* p. 100. For a characteristically sound discussion see R. MacMullen, *The Roman Government's Response to Crisis,* pp. 6–26.

18. *Digest* 39, 6, 3–5.

19. A. D. Momigliano, "Seneca," *Quarto contributo alla storia degli studi classici e del mondo antico* (Rome, 1969), p. 255.

20. R. Syme, *Emperors and Biographers* (Oxford, 1971), p. 181.

21. *Pap. Oxy.* 1477; M. Rostovtzeff, *The Social and Economic History of the Roman Empire* (Oxford, 1926), p. 427. The problems raised were by no means confined to the third century: see A. Henrichs, "Zwei Orakelfragen," *Zeitschrift f. Papyrologie und Epigraphik* 11 (1973), 117.

22. Marcus Aurelius, *Meditations* IV, 32.

23. See the wise remarks of R. Gordon, "Mithraism and Roman Society," *Religion* 2 (1972), 92.

24. Plutarch, *De defectu orac.* 421 A.

25. This is true even for the most ostensibly "non-Roman" and aggressively missionary religious movement in Late Antiquity, Manichaeism. See Peter Brown, "The Diffusion of Manichaeism in the Roman Empire." *Journal of Roman Studies* 59 (1969), 92–103 = *Religion and Society*, pp. 94–118.

26. H. I. Marrou, *Histoire de l'education dans l'antiquité*, 6th ed. (Paris, 1965), p. 300.

27. L. Bieler, *Theios Anēr* (Vienna, 1935), p. 3: "Die Spätantike, die dem frühen Griechentum in mehr als einer Hinsicht verwandt war."

28. τὰ ἀνθρωποπρεπῆ μου νόμιμα ἐκτελέσαι: *P. Monac.* 8, 5–6, cited in E. Wipszicka, *Les ressources et les activités économiques des églises en Egypte* (Brussels, 1972), p. 30; discussed in E. F. Bruck, *Totenteil und Seelengerät im griechischen Recht* (Munich, 1926), pp. 302–304.

29. Plato, *Laws* IV, 716 D.

30. Origen, *In Gen.* 10, 1.

31. A. D. Nock, "The Milieu of Gnosticism," *Gnomon* 12 (1936), 612 = *Essays on Religion and the Ancient World*, ed. Z. Stewart (Oxford 1972), p. 451. Underemployment was chronic in the Mediterranean world. See Artemidorus, *Oneirocriticon*, ed. R. Pack (Leipzig, Teubner, 1963), I, 32, 41.1; I, 54, 61.2; I, 64, 70.12; I, 81, 98.18–99.6; II, 3, 102.17, 104.7, 104.20; II, 55, 184.6, for dreams foretelling loss of work. The soldier is an enviable exception: II, 31, 154.12: οὔτε γὰρ ἀργὸς ὁ στρατιώτης οὔτε ἐνδεής ἐστι. See E. Patlagean, *Pauvreté économique et pauvreté sociale à Byzance*, pp. 169–170.

32. R. Syme, *Ammianus and the Historia Augusta* (Oxford, 1968), p. 31.

33. A. H. M. Jones, *The Later Roman Empire* (Oxford, 1964), II, 975. Well appreciated by A. Merklein, *Das Ehescheidungsrecht nach den Papyri der byzantinischen Zeit* (Erlangen, 1967), pp. 73–79 at p. 79: "Man wollte mit Hilfe der Dämonenformel die gesamte Vorgeschichte der Scheidung elegant übergehen."

34. See the classic account of the impingement of witchcraft beliefs: E. E. Evans-Pritchard, *Witchcraft, Oracles and Magic among the Azande* (Oxford, 1937), pp. 63–83.

35. A. D. Nock, "Studies in the Graeco-Roman Beliefs of the Empire," *Journal of Hellenic Studies* 45 (1925), 85 = *Essays on Religion and the Ancient World*, p. 35.

36. Peter Brown, "The Rise and Function of the Holy Man in Late Antiquity," *Journal of Roman Studies* 61 (1972), 80–101.

37. R. Draguet, "Une lettre de Serapion de Thmuis aux disciples d'Antoine." *Le Mouseon* 64 (1951), chap. 5, p. 13.

38. Arnobius, *Adv. Gentes* I, 51: *Transcribere posse in hominem ius tuum: quod facere solus possis, fragilissimae rei donare, participare faciendum.*

39. Augustine, *De civ. Dei* V, 26, 11, and *De cura gerenda pro mortuis* xvii, 21; Palladius, *Historia Lausiaca* 35.

40. Theodoret, *Historia religiosa*, P. G. 82. 1481 A.

41. εἶδον εἰκόνα τοῦ Ἰακώβου ᾽Αθήνησι καὶ μοι ἔδοξεν ὁ ἀνὴρ εὐφυὴς μὲν οὐ πάνυ εἶναι σεμνὸς δὲ καὶ ἐμβριθής: Damascius, *Vitae Isidori reliquiae*, ed. C. Zintzen. (Hildeshem, 1967), 124, p. 168, 10; H. P. L'Orange, *Apotheosis in Ancient Portraiture* (Oslo, 1947); H. von Heintze, "*Vir gravis et sanctus*, Bildniskopf eines spätantiken Philosophen," *Jahrb. f. Antike und Christentum* 6 (1963), 35–53.

42. A. D. Momigliano, "Pagan and Christian Historiography in the Fourth Century A.D.," *The Conflict between Paganism and Christianity in the Fourth Century* (Oxford 1963), p. 93.

43. μισεῖν τὸ σεμνὸν καὶ τὸ μὴ πᾶσιν φίλον: Euripides, *Hippolytus* 93.

44. Peter Brown, "The Rise and Function of the Holy Man," *Journal of Roman Studies* 61 (1972), 97–100.

45. E. R. Dodds, *Pagan and Christian*, pp. 6–7.

46. Optatus of Milevis, *De schismate Donatistarum* II, 22: *Si ad vos divina migravit de caelo religio.*

47. *Exod. rabbah, Wa'era* xii, 4.

48. Cyprian, *Ep.* 11, 6: *sublime iam pectus.*

49. Eusebius, *Demonstratio Evangelica* VI, 8.

50. Eusebius, *Vita Constantini*, IV, 15.

51. Jerome, *Ep.* 23, 3.

52. *Monumenta Asiae Minoris Antiqua* VIII (Manchester, 1962) no. 487, p. 104; see L. Robert, *Hellenica* 13 (1965), 170.

53. *Corpus Inscriptionum Latinarum* XIII, 2395.

54. Heliodorus, *Aethiopica* III, 16.

55. Οὐκ ἔστιν αὕτη ἡ σοφία ἄνωθεν κατερχομένη ἀλλ᾽ ἐπίγειος ψυχικὴ δαιμονιώδης: *Epistle of James* 3, 15. Cf. Hermas, *Pastor*, Mand. XI, 43, 5–6.

56. *The Testament of our Lord*, II, 7, trans. J. Cooper and A. J. Maclean (Edinburgh, 1902), p. 123.

57. See Eunapius, *Lives of the Sophists*, 474: ὅτι δὲ τὴν αἴσθησιν ἀπατῶσαι μαγγανεῖαι καὶ γοητεύουσαι, θαυματοποιῶν ἔργα, καὶ πρὸς ὑλικὰς τινας δυνάμεις παραποιοντων καὶ μεμηνότων. It is exceedingly difficult to translate this passage without importing into it a modern distinction between philosophical thought which is "real," in our sense, and magic which is "unreal" in our sense of "nonexistent." This is not how Eunapius would have seen it; see below p. 61.

58. Koran, *Sura 54*, 3. For an extensive and subtle discussion of the issues raised by miracles in Muslim circles see Abu Bakr ibn al-Ṭaiyib, al-Baqilani (d. 1031), *Al-Bayān 'an al-farq bain al-mu'jizāt wa'l-karāmāt wa'l-ḥiyal wa'l-kahānah wa'l-siḥr wa'l-nāranjāt* (Miracle and magic: A treatise on the nature of the apologetic miracle and its differentiation from charisms, trickery, divination, magic and spells), ed. Richard J. McCarthy, University of Baghdad, Silsilat 'Ilm al-Kalam, II (Beirut, 1958), esp. chaps. 29–35, pp. 26–31, English summary, p. 16, and chap. 70, pp. 59–60; summary, p. 20.

59. Augustine, *De utilitate credendi* xvi, 34.

60. Plutarch, *De defectu orac.* 415A.

61. H. Wey, *Die Funktionen der bösen Geister bei den griechischen Apologeten des 2. Jahrh. n. Chr.* (Winterthur, 1957), sees very clearly the evolution that takes place, possibly under Christian influence, between Plutarch and Porphyry.

62. Plutarch, *De defectu orac.* 416E: on the Moon as an "anomalous" mixture: μεικτὸν δὲ σῶμα καὶ δαιμόνιον. See the evidence now collected, with little attempt at interpretation, s.v. "Geister," *Reallexikon f. Antike and Christentum* IX (Stuttgart, 1975), 546–797, and below pp. 74–75.

63. *Demonstratio Evangelica* III, 6, *P.G.* 22.224.

64. Galen, *Method, med.* I, 3, Kühn X, 29.

65. Paulus, *Sententiae* V, 21, 1; Digest L 13, 1, 3.

66. Plotinus, *Enneads* II, 9, 14.

67. Charles Pietri, *Roma Christiana*, Bibliothèque de l'Ecole française d'Athènes et Rome, 224, 2 (Rome, 1976), pp. 1558–1562.

68. *The Acts of Thomas.* 20, trans. A. F. J. Klijn (Leiden 1962), p. 74. Cf. Ibn Khaldun, *The Muqaddimah: An Introduction to History*, trans. Franz Rosenthal, III (London, 1967), 167: "We, however, (prefer to) deduce the differentiation merely from obvious signs. That is, miracles are found (to be wrought) by good persons for good purposes and by souls that are entirely devoted to good deeds . . . Sorcery, on the other hand, is found (practised) only by evil persons and as a rule is used for evil actions."

69. S. Calderone, "Ideologia politica, successione dinastica e consecratio in età costantiniana," *Le culte des souverains*, Entretiens de la Fondation Hardt, XIX (Geneva, 1975), p. 227: "Per questa visione piramidale del mondo, Eusebio ripeteva l'idea che da piu un secolo aveva preso a dominare il pensiero antico. La parola d'ordine del 3o. secolo . . . fu *monarchia*."

70. E.g., Jamblichus, *De mysteriis* I, 5, 17.8–20; see esp. John Dillon, *Iamblichi Chalcidensis in Platonis dialogos fragmenta* (Leiden, 1973), pp. 407–411.

71. E.g., Augustine, *De civ. Dei* X, 15–17.

72. Excellent examples of the traditional appearances of gods and heroes in dreams to warn their worshipers can be found in *Monumenta Asiae Minoris Antiqua* IV (Manchester 1933) no. 279, 10, p. 105, and P. Herrmann, "Das Testament des Epikrates," *Österreichische Akademie der Wissenschaften*, Phil.-Hist. Kl. 265, 1 (Vienna, 1969), p. 10, line 33.

73. This does not exclude "designation" of a human being by the god in an oracle, e.g., *Année Épigraphique* 1972, no. 591, but this is hardly surprising for a συγγένιδα συνκλητικῶν καὶ ἀσιαρχῶν. Cf. A. D. Nock, "A Diis Electa," *Harvard Theological Review* 23 (1936), 251–274, esp. p. 255 = *Essays*, p. 256, and L. Robert, *Hellenica* 11–12 (1960), 463 ff. See also James Wiseman, "Gods, War and Plague in the Time of the Antonines," *Studies in the Antiquities of Stobi* (Belgrade, 1973), pp. 152–183 at p. 153.

74. Celsus apud Origen, *Contra Celsum* VIII, 45.

75. Lucian, *Alexander* 29 and 43.

76. J. Guey, "Encore la 'Pluie miraculeuse,'" *Revue de Philologie* 22 (1948), 16–62.

77. Galen, *De praenotione* 1, Kühn XIV, 603.

78. Polemo, *Physiognomica*, ed. R. Foerster, trans. C. Hoffman (Leipzig, Teubner, 1893), p. 162.8.

79. Apuleius, *Apologia* 25.

80. Origen, *Contra Celsum* VII, 41.

81. Marcus Aurelius, *Meditations* I, 6.

82. Galen, *De cognosc. anim. morb.* 3, Kühn V, 10–11.

83. Lucian, *Vit. auct.* 2.

84. Lucian, *Alexander* 26.

85. Lucian, *Peregrinus* 12.

86. H. D. Betz, *Lukian von Samosata und das Neue Testament*, Texte und Untersuchungen 76 (Berlin, 1961), pp. 100–101.

87. Lucian, *Demonax* 64.

88. Lucian, *Demonax* 63.

89. H. Wiegartz, *Kleinasiatische Säulensarkophage* (Berlin, 1965), p. 121.

90. G. Rodenwaldt, "Zur Kunstgeschichte der Jahre 220 bis 270," *Romische Mitteilungen* 51 (1936), 82–113 at p. 93, and G. M. A. Hanfmann, *The Season Sarcophagus in Dumbarton Oaks*, I (Cambridge, Mass., 1951), 237–238.

2 AN AGE OF AMBITION

1. Edward Gibbon, *Decline and Fall of the Roman Empire*, chap. 2 (London, 1888), p. 76.

2. S. Mazzarino, *The End of the Ancient World*, trans. G. Holmes (London, 1966), p. 130.

3. A. J. Festugière, *La Révélation d'Hermès Trismégiste*, I (Paris, 1950), 4.

4. E. L. Bowie, "The Greeks and Their Past in the Second Sophistic," *Past and Present* 46 (1970), 3–41.

5. R. Syme, *Emperors and Biographers* (Oxford, 1971), p. 181.

6. H. Lechat, *Epidaure* (Paris, 1895), p. 153.

7. Glen Bowersock, *Greek Sophists in the Roman Empire* (Oxford, 1969), p. 73: "Aristides was more characteristic of his age than many admirers of it would like to think." Cf. E. R. Dodds, *Pagan and Christian*, pp. 40–45.

8. J. Geffcken, *Der Ausgang des griechisch-römischen Heidentums* (Heidelberg, 1929), pp. 20–30. Translated with updated footnotes by S. G. MacCormack, *The Last Days of Greco-Roman Paganism* (Amsterdam, 1978).

9. E.g., W. H. C. Frend, *Martyrdom and Persecution in the Early Church* (Oxford, 1965), pp. 440–476.

10. S. Mazzarino, *Aspetti sociali del quarto secolo* (Rome, 1951), pp. 217–269.

11. P. Petit, *Libanius et la vie municipale à Antioche* (Paris, 1955); W. Liebeschütz, *Antioch: City and Imperial Administration in the Later Roman Empire* (Oxford, 1972), and G. L. Kurbatov, *Osnovnye problemy vnutrennego razvitija vizantiiskogo goroda* (Leningrad, 1971).

12. A. P. Février, "Ostie de Porto à la fin de l'antiquité: Topographie religieuse et vie sociale," *Mél d'Archéologie et d'Histoire* 70 (1957–58), 295–330; "Notes sur le développement urbain en Afrique du Nord," *Cahiers Archéologiques* 14 (1964), 1–47; and "Permanence et héritages de l'antiquité dans la topographie des villes de l'occident," *Settimane di Studi sull'Alto Medio Evo* 21.1 (Spoleto, 1974), 41–138.

13. Clive Foss, *Late Roman and Byzantine Sardis* (Cambridge, Mass. 1976), pp. 39–57; G. M. A. Hanfmann, *From Croesus to Constantine* (Ann Arbor, 1975); the dossier in D. Claude, *Die byzantinische Stadt im 6. Jahrhundert*, Byzantinisches Archiv 13 (Munich, 1969); and A. M. Mansel, "Die Grabbauten von Side (Pamphylien)," *Jahrbuch d. deutsch. archäologischen Instituts* 74 (1959), 363–402.

14. The role of the city in North Africa had received special attention from T. Kotula, "Snobisme municipal ou prospérité relative? Recherches sur le statut municipal des villes nord-africaines sous le bas-empire romain," *Antiquités Africaines* 8 (1974), 111–131, and *Afryka północna w starożytności* (Wrocław, 1972), pp. 342–385. Cf. C. Lepelley, "Saint Augustin et la cité romano-africaine," *Jean Chrysostome et Augustin*, ed. C. Kannengiesser (Paris, 1975), pp. 13–39. For further

evidence of continuous restoration in the fourth century: A. Beschouach, "Tremblement de terre et prospérité économique," *Comptesrendus de l'Acad. des inscriptions et belles lettres* (1975), pp. 101 ff. On the danger of interpreting the construction of city walls as exclusively a symptom of crisis: René Rebuffat, "Enceintes urbaines et insecurité en Maurétanie Tingitane," *Mélanges d'Archéologie et d'Histoire. Antiquité* 86 (1974), 501–522.

15. G. Bowersock, *Greek Sophists*, p. 29.

16. R. MacMullen, *Roman Social Relations* (New Haven, 1974), p. 61.

17. A. Boulanger, *Aelius Aristide* (Paris, 1923), p. 11: on Asia—"dans ce pays où la pierre bavarde."

18. Philostratus, *Life of Apollonius of Tyana* IV, 8: ὁμονοίας στασιαζούσης δεῖσθαι.

19. R. MacMullen, *Roman Social Relations*, p. 125, and he adds, to our shame: "So far as I know, it has yet to receive the compliment of a scholarly treatise."

20. L. Robert, *Hellenica* 13 (1965), 224: "Πλουσίως. La cité grecque n'eût pas employé ce mot."

21. Galen, *De cognosc. anim. morb.* 9, Kühn V, 50. Cf. on Opromoas, *Tituli Asiae Minoris*, vol: II, pt. 3 (Vienna, 1944), no. 905, IIF, 12, p. 329: ἐν μὲν τῇ πατρίδι πρῶτον, ἐν δὲ τῷ ἔθνει ἐκ τῶν πρωτευόντων.

22. E.g., the evidence in P. Garnsey, *Social Status and Legal Privilege in the Roman Empire* (Oxford, 1971), and his brilliant study, "Aspects of the Decline of the Urban Aristocracy in the Empire," *Aufstieg und Niedergang d. Römischen Welt* 2.1 (Berlin, 1974), 229–252.

23. F. Millar, *The Emperor in the Roman World*, p. 420.

24. Plutarch, *Praecepta ger. reipub.* c. 19, 814F–815A.

25. Philostratus, *Lives of the Sophists*, II, 1, 559–563; see Millar, *The Emperor in the Roman World*, pp. 4–5.

26. Ammianus Marcellinus, *Res gestae* XXX, 4, 9–10.

27. Plutarch, *De tranquill. animi*, c. 10, 470 C; see Millar, *The Emperor in the Roman World*, p. 300.

28. A. H. M. Jones, *The Later Roman Empire*, II, 737–763.

29. G. Bowersock, *Greek Sophists*, pp. 17–29; the architecture tells the same tale—lavish construction in a uniform style, but by local craftsmen for local donors: M. Lyttleton, *Baroque Architecture in Classical Antiquity* (London, 1974), p. 271.

30. P. Pouthier, "Evolution municipale d'Altava aux iiième et ivème siècle," *Mél. d'archéol. et d'histoire* 68 (1956), 205–245 at p. 213.

31. P. Garnsey, "Aspects of the Decline of the Urban Aristocracy," *Aufstieg und Niedergang*, 2.1, 240.

32. E. Benz, "Der 'Übermensch'—Begriff in der Theologie der alten Kirche." *Texte und Untersuchungen* 77 (Berlin, 1961), 135–160 at p. 144: "Der Tod erscheint hier wie in den mittelalterlichen Totentänzen als der grosse Demokrat."

33. Plutarch, *De deo Socratis* 9, 579F: οἱ δὲ ὡς θεοφιλεῖς καὶ περιττοί τινες εἶναι δοκοῖεν ἐπιθειάξουσι τὰς πράξεις, ὀνείρατα καὶ φάσματα καὶ τοιοῦτον ἄλλον ὄγκον προΐσταμενοι. Cf. A. Guillaume, *The Life of Mohammed* (Oxford 1952), pp. 142–143: "What did I hear! We and the Banu Abdu-Manaf have been rivals in honour. They have fed the poor, so have we; they have assumed others' burdens, so have we; they have been generous, so have we, until we have squatted on your knees face to face (as complete equals) as if we were like two horses of equal speed. They said 'We have a Prophet to whom revelation comes from Heaven,' and when shall we attain anything like that? By God, we will not believe in him or treat him as truthful."

34. O. Neugebauer and H. B. van Hoesen, *Greek Horoscopes* (Philadelphia, 1959), p. 97.

35. M. Berthelot, *Collection des anciens alchimistes grecs* (Paris, 1887).

36. E. H. Gombrich, *Norm and Form* (London, 1966), pp. 35–37.

37. Plutarch, *Praecepta ger. reipub.* c. 30, 822 B.

38. See above p. 23.

39. See the chilling description of the onset and course of an earthquake in Pausanias, *Description of Greece* VII, 24, 6–11.

40. On the activity of Opromoas, publicized in extraordinary detail around his mausoleum: *Tituli Asiae Minoris*, vol. II, pl. 3, no. 905, XIVE, 7, p. 341, and L. Robert, *Hellenica* 12 (1965), 544. Persecution of the Christians may have coincided with earth tremors: Eusebius, *Hist. Eccl.* IV, 13; but see T. D. Barnes, *Journal of Roman Studies* 58 (1968), 38.

41. Eusebius, *Praeparatio Evangelica* IV, 1; K. Buresch, *Claros, Untersuchungen z. Orakelwesen d. späteren Antike* (Leipzig, 1889), p. 35. For a recent example of an unexceptionable oracle, naming Athena as the "helper of cities" see Thomas Drew-Bear and W. D. Lebek, "An Oracle of Apollo at Miletus," *Greek, Roman and Byzantine Studies* 14 (1973), 65–73. Cf. R. Thouvenot, "Un oracle d'Apollon de Claros à Volubilis," *Bull. d'Archeol. Marocaine* 8 (1968/72), 221–227.

42. This is well demonstrated by L. Robert, *Hellenica* 11–12 (1960), 546: "La prospérité des oracles s'explique par l'inquiétude religieuse, et l'oracle tend à l'apaiser, à la canaliser."

43. M. West, "Oracles of Apollo Kareios: A Revised Text," *Zeitschrift für Papyrologie und Epigraphik* 1 (1967), 183–187, at p. 187 —West's summary of a fragmentary text.

44. Plutarch, *De Pyth. orac.* 25, 407C; Lucian, *Alexander* 30.

45. K. Buresch, *Claros*, p. 39; "Iao war zeitgemäss und von keinem klugen Apollo mehr zu leugnen."

46. Oracles on the approaching end of Christianity and activity at oracle sites: H. Bloch, "A New Document of the last Pagan Revival' in the West," *Harvard Theological Review* 38 (1945), 199–202 and 234 ff., and Augustine *De civ. Dei* XVIII, 53; Zachariah of Mitylene, *Vie de Sévère, Patrologia Orientalis* 2.1, 40.

47. Origen, *In Matth. ad c.* 24, 9–14: *sed et qui videbantur prudentes, talia in publico dicerent, quia propter Christianos fiunt gravissimae terrae motus.* Marc le Diacre, *Vie de Porphyre* 19, ed. H. Grégoire and M. A. Kugener (Paris, 1930), p. 16, on the drought at Gaza in 396: καὶ ἐπέγραφον πάντες οἱ ἀπὸ τῆς πόλεως τὸ πρᾶγμα τῷ ἐισόδῳ τοῦ μακαρίου λέγοντες ὅτι Ἐχρηματίσθη ἡμῖν ὑπὸ τοῦ Μαρνοῦ ὅτι κακοποδινός ἐστιν ὁ Πορφύριος τῇ πόλει.

48. Fergus Millar, "P. Herennius Dexippus: The Greek World, and the Third Century Invasions," *Journal of Roman Studies* 59 (1969). 12–29 at p. 13.

49. Thomas Hobbes, *Leviathan* I, xi.

50. Artemidorus, *Oneirocriticon*, IV, 44, p. 271, trans. R. White, *The Interpretation of Dreams: The Oneirocritica of Artemidorus*, Noyes Classical Studies (Park Ridge, N.J.), p. 203.

51. E.g., Marcus Aurelius, *Meditations* 1,15. Cf. *Fronto to Appian*, ed. C. R. Haines, Loeb Classical Library (Cambridge, Mass., 1919), pp. 269–279; ed. M. P. J. van den Hout (Leiden, 1954), pp. 228–223.

52. See E. A. Thompson, *The Historical Work of Ammianus Marcellinus* (Cambridge, 1947), pp. 82–83. Like Ammianus, Thompson is unduly harsh on this aspect of Julian.

53 On the importance of πρᾳότης ascribed (wishfully) to governors in the Later Empire see L. Robert, *Hellenica* 13 (1965), 223–224.

54. E.g., Maximus of Tyre, *Diss.* XIV, 6: ὁ μὲν εὐσεβῆς φίλος θεοῦ, ὁ δὲ δεισιδαίμων κόλαξ θεοῦ.

55. Galen, *De cognosc. anim. morb.* 4, Kühn V, 16, trans. Paul W. Harkins, *On the Passions and Errors of the Soul* (Columbia, 1963).

56. Galen, *De cognosc. anim. morb.* 4, Kühn V, 17.

57. Galen, *De cognosc. anim. morb.* 4, Kühn V, 19.

58. Galen, *De cognosc. anim. morb.* 8, Kühn V, 40–41.

59. Philostratus, *Lives of the Sophists* 526.

60. Artemidorus, *Oneirocriticon* III, 53, p. 227.10.

61. Artemidorus, *Oneirocriticon* I, 13, p. 21.13–22.18.

62. Artemidorus, *Oneirocriticon* I, 68, p. 192.1.

63. Artemidorus, *Oneirocriticon* I, 50, p. 55.12.

64. Artemidorus, *Oneirocriticon* I, 77, p. 86.2.

65. Gabriel Michenaud and Jean Dierkens, *Le rêve dans les "Discours Sacrés" d'Aelius Aristide* (Mons, 1972).

66. Apuleius, *Apologia* 55.

67. Apuleius, *Metamorphoses* XI, 19.

68. Aelius Aristides, Περὶ τοῦ Παραφθέγματος 392, ed. W. Dindorf (Leipzig, 1829), II, 529, referring to *Sacred Tales* IV, 52.

69. Aelius Aristides, Περὶ τοῦ Παραφθέγματος 387, Dindorf II, 518.

70. Philostratus, *Lives of the Sophists*, 535.

71. Aelius Aristides, Εἰς Ἀσκλήπιον 39, Dindorf, I, 67, *Sacred Tales* IV, 27, trans. C. A. Behr (Amsterdam, 1968), p. 259.

72. Galen, *De sanitate tuenda*, I, 8, Kühn VI, 41-42.

73. Aelius Aristides, *Sacred Tales* II, 21-22, Behr, p. 227.

74. Aelius Aristides, *Sacred Tales* III, 5, Behr, p. 242; IV, 17, Behr, p. 257.

75. Aelius Aristides, *Sacred Tales* III, 38, Behr, p. 249.

76. Aelius Aristides, *Sacred Tales* III, 43, Behr, p. 250: ὅπῶς μὴ δοκοίην δημοκοπικός τις.

77. Aelius Aristides, *Sacred Tales* I, 59, Behr, p. 218.

78. Galen, *In Hipp. praedict.* I, 5, Kühn XV1, 525: διὰ τὴν ξηρότητα πάντη ἐναργῆ φαίνεται τὰ κατὰ τοὺς ὕπνους φάσματα.

79. Tertullian, *De ieiunio* I, 4.

80. Herodian, *History* III, 2, 7-8. See Fergus Millar, *The Emperor in the Roman World* (London, 1977), pp. 416-417.

81. Herodian, *History* VII, 8, 2.

82. Herodian, *History* VI, 8, 4: Alexander Severus loses support: πάσης προανηλωμένης φιλοτιμίας.

83. *Mekilta* II, 229ff. Cf. Basil of Caesarea, *Hom. in Ps.* LXI, 4, *P.G.* 29.477, where the urban benefactor provides identical services.

84. *Année Épigraphique* 1972, nos. 626, 627, 628.

85. K. T. Erim and Joyce Reynolds, "A Letter of Gordian III from Aphrodisias in Caria," *Journal of Roman Studies* 59 (1969), 56-58. See F. Millar, *The Emperor in the Roman World*, p. 417.

86. Fritz Gschnitzer and Josef Keil, "Neue Inschriften aus Lydien," *Anz. österr. Akad. Wiss.* 93 (1956), 219-232 at p. 228.

87. It was the same with the restriction of the number of bishoprics: *Conc. Serdica*, canon 6: ἵνα μὴ κατευτελίξηται τὸ τοῦ ἐπισκόπου ὄνομα καὶ ἡ αὐθεντία.

88. F. Bruns and T. Mommsen, *Fontes iuris romani antiqui* (Berlin, 1909), 97b, p. 270.

89. W. Dittenberger, *Sylloge Inscriptionum Graecarum* II (Leipzig, 1917), p. 622, no. 904: φόβος καὶ ἄγνοια τῶν δικαζομένων ἐξηρήσθω; and

no. 905, p. 623 : ὑπὲρ τοῦ μηδεμίαν ὑμᾶς τῶν ὁρισθέντων ἄγνοιαν προβάλλεσθαι, βρέβιον τῶν εἰρημένων ἁπάντων ἀκρειβῆ διδασκαλίαν ἐπέχον.

90. J. P. Callu, *La politique monétaire des empereurs romains de 238 à 311* (Paris, 1969), p. 483.

91. This has been well demonstrated in the area of panegyric by S. G. MacCormack, "Latin Prose Panegyrics: Tradition and Discontinuity in the Later Roman Empire," *Revue des Études Augustiniennes* 22 (1976), 29–77, esp. at pp. 53–54. On the continuity of a Classical legal tradition on which Diocletian built: G. Schnebelt, *Reskripte der Soldatenkaiser* (Karlsruhe, 1974).

92. M. A. Wes, "Patrocinium en imperium in het laat-Romeinse Westen," *Tijdschrift voor Geschiedenis* 87 (1974), 147–159 at pp. 157–158.

93. H. F. Pflaum, *Les Procurateurs équestres* (Paris, 1950), p. 66.

94. E.g., *Bull. corr. hell.* 12 (1888), 101, no. 22.9 : πρὸς μὲν τοὺς θεοὺς εὐσεβῶς, πρὸς δὲ τοὺς ἀνθρώπους φιλοτείμως.

95. Compare the equilibrium of criteria of status implied in earlier inscriptions : *Bull. corr. hell.* 12. 11 (1888), 88 : φιλοκαίσαρα καὶ φιλόπατριν θεοφιλῆς.

96. See the literature at no. 12 above.

97. On Majorinus see A. H. M. Jones, J. R. Martindale, and J. Morris, *The Prosopography of the Later Roman Empire* (Cambridge, 1971), pp. 437–538, and D. Levi, *Antioch Mosaic Pavements* (Princeton, 1947), p. 1, lxxix. On Africa, see M. Blanchard-Lamée, *Maison à mosaiques du quartier central de Djemila* (Paris, 1976), p. 237.

98. Cassiodorus, *Variae* III, 9 and VI, 44. (I owe the reference to the kindness of Brian Ward-Perkins.) For Rome in the fifth century see J. F. Matthews, *Western Aristocracies and Imperial Court* (Oxford, 1975), pp. 356–357. In Constantinople this was controlled : *Cod. Just.* VIII, xi, 20 (A.D. 439). On the survival of public places in the towns of the Eastern Empire, see D. Claude, *Die byzantinische Stadt*, pp. 60–69.

99. M. Meslin, *La fête des kalendes de janvier dans l'empire romain*, Collection Latomus 115 (Brussels, 1970).

100. A. D. Nock, "The Augustan Restoration," *Classical Review* 39 (1925), 60–67 = *Essays*, pp. 16–25; J. Geffcken, *Der Ausgang*, pp. 28–30.

101. Lactantius, *De mort. persec.* XI, 7; H. Grégoire, "Les Chrétiens et l'oracle de Didymes," *Mél. Holleaux* (Paris, 1913), pp. 81–91, and *Byzantion* 14 (1939), 321.

102. B. Brenk, "Die Datierung der Reliefs am Hadrianstempel und das Problem der tetrarchischen Skulpturen des Ostens," *Istanbuler Mitteilungen* 18 (1968), 238–258, esp. p. 251: "Damit wird dem

Glauben an die aktive Präsenz der Götter in der Geschichte Ausdruck verleihen."

103. Ibid., p. 250.

104. *Année Epgraphique* 1972, no. 666.

105. Eusebius, *Praeparatio evangelica* IV. 2. The prophet at Miletus was also involved. *Hist. Eccles.* IX, 2, i–iii, on Theotecnus in Antioch.

106. A Laumonier, *Les cultes indigènes de la Carie* (Paris, 1958) p. 288, n1: "une continuité et une stabilité remarquables."

107. *Bull. corr. hell.* 12 (1888), 101; Dittenberger, *Sylloge*, no. 900, pp. 616–619.

108. Fergus Millar, "P. Herennius Dexippus," *Journal of Roman Studies* 59 (1969), 16–19.

109. E.g., Eunapius of Sardis, *Lives of the Sophists* pp. 481–482, says that Priscus "was of too secretive a disposition, and his learning was recondite and abstruse ... His bearing was deliberate and lofty ... maintaining at all times a secretive manner and sneering at human weakness." See H. D. Saffrey and L. G. Westerink, *Proclus: Théologie platonicienne* (Paris, 1968), pp. xxxv–xlviii.

110. Zosimus, *Historia Nova* IV, 18.

111. Julian, *Misopogon* 361A–362A.

112. John H. Humphrey, "Prolegomena to the Study of the Hippodrome at Caesarea," *Bull. Amer. School of Oriental Research* 213 (1974), 2–45, and V. Popović and E. L. Ochsenslager, "Der spätkaiserzeitliche Hippodrom in Sirmium," *Germania* 54 (1976), 156–181. On the racing at Daphnae in the sixth century, see Severus of Antioch *Homily* LIV, *Patrologia Orientalis* IV, 50.

113. John Chrysostom, *On Vainglory* 4, ed. B. K. Exarchos (Munich, 1953), p. 36, trans. M. L. W. Laistner, *Christianity and Pagan Culture* (Ithaca, 1951), p. 87.

114. Theodosius II in the Hippodrome: John Rufus, *Plerophoriae* 99, *Patrologia Orientalis* VIII, 173.30. G. Dagron, *Naissance d'une capitale: Constantinople* (Paris, 1974), pp. 320–347, esp. p. 346. The connection between the successes of the racing colors and the *Tyché* of the Empire continued in the Middle Ages. When the Blues win, the Empire will defeat the Muslims; when the Greens win, the Muslims will be successful, and robes of honor are distributed to the Muslim prisoners: Muqaddasi, *Ahsan at-taqāsīm*, p. 148, cited in A. Miquel, *La géographie humaine du monde musulman*, II (Paris, 1975), 477. See Alan Cameron, *Circus Factions* (Oxford, 1976), pp. 157–192, and 201–234.

3 THE RISE OF THE FRIENDS OF GOD

1. *Mart. Polycarp.* 5, 2, ed. tr. H. Musurillo, *The Acts of the Christian Martyrs* (Oxford, 1972), p. 6. I use this, in many ways inadequate, edition for convenience only.

2. Pontius, *Vita Cypriani* 12.

3. Aelius Aristides, *Sacred Tales* II, 20–23, Behr, pp. 227–228.

4. *Mart. Polycarp.* 13, 2, Musurillo, p. 12.

5. Lucian, *Peregrinus* 37.

6. *Mart. Polycarp.* 15, 2, Musurillo, p. 14.

7. *Mart. Polycarp.* 17, 1, Musurillo, p. 14.

8. *Mart. Pion.* 20, 6, Musurillo, p. 162.

9. Edward Gibbon, *The Decline and Fall*, chap. 15 (London, 1888) p. 31.

10. *Martyrs of Lyons*, Eusebius, *Hist. Eccl.* V, 1, 20, Musurillo, p. 68: "He kept repeating this again and again instead of giving his name, birthplace, nationality, or anything else."

11. *Mart. Polycarp.* 2, Musurillo, p. 2: μᾶλλον δὲ ὅτι παρεστὼς ὁ Κύριος ὡμίλει αὐτοῖς.

12. *Passio Perpetuae* 16, Musurillo, p. 124: *verebatur ne subtrahantur de carcere incantationibus magicis.*

13. *Mart. Pion.* 13, 4–5, Musurillo, p. 152. Cf. A. D. Nock, *Sallustius: Concerning the Gods and the Universe* (Cambridge, 1926), p. xcii, n217, on the βιαιοθανής.

14. A. von Harnack, *Mission and Ausbreitung des Christentums* (2d ed. Leipzig, 1906) trans. as *Mission and Expansion of Christianity* (rev. ed. London, 1908); see B. Kötting, s.v. "Christentum: Ausbreitung," *Reallexikon f. antike ul Christentum* II (Stuttgart, 1954), 1138–1159.

15. See the excellent survey of W. Zeisel, Jr., "An Economic Survey of the Early Byzantine Church" (Ph.D. dissertation, Rutgers University, 1975).

16. Origen, *Contra Celsum* III, 55; it should be pointed out that Galen ascribed an identical appeal to the vulgar in his professional rivals: *Method. med.* 1, Kühn, X, 5: διὰ τοῦτο καὶ σκυτότομοι καὶ τέκτονες καὶ βαφεῖς καὶ χαλκεῖς ἐπιτηδῶσιν ἤδη τοῖς ἔργοις τῆς ἰατρικῆς . . . καὶ περὶ πρωτείων ἐρίξουσι.

17. T. D. Barnes, *Tertullian* (Oxford, 1971), and "Tertullian the Antiquarian," *Texte und Untersuchungen* 117 (Berlin, 1976), 3–20.

18. S. Mazzarino, "Religione ed economia sotto Commodo e i Severi," *Antico, tardoantico ed èra costantiniana* (Rome, 1974), pp. 51–73; H. Gülzow "Kallist von Rom. Ein Beitrag z. Soziologie d. röm. Gemeinde," *Zeitschr. f. neutest. Wiss.* 58 (1968), 102–121.

19. M. M. Sage, *Cyprian*, Patristic Monographs Series I (Greene, Hadden and Co., Cambridge, Mass., 1975).

20. Fergus Millar, "Paul of Samosata, Zenobia and Aurelian: The Church, Local Culture and Political Allegiance in the Third Century," *Journal of Roman Studies* 61 (1971), 1–17.

21. *Pap. Oxy.* 2673.

22. Lucian, *Vit. auct.* 2.

23. Eunapius, *Lives of the Sophists* 474.

24. E. R. Dodds, "Theurgy and Its Relationship to Neo-Platonism," *Journal of Roman Studies* 37 (1947) 55–69; Jeannie Carlier, "Science divine et raison humaine," in *Divination et rationalité* by J. P. Vernant and others (Paris, 1974), pp. 249–263, esp. p. 258.

25. Eunapius, *Lives* 477.

26. Ibid., 504.

27. N. H. Baynes in a letter to A. D. Nock, cited in A. D. Nock, "A Diis Electa," *Harvard Theological Review* 23 (1930) 264 = *Essays*, 262 Cf. André Piganiol, *L'empire chrétien* (Paris, 1972), p. 78, "Si Constantin avait été . . . calculateur, il n'aurait pas exécuté sa grande oeuvre. Pour y réussir il fallait un inspiré." This "inspiration" was assumed to govern and to validate day-to-day political maneuvering. The conspiracy of Maximin against him was revealed to Constantine and duly suppressed: παραδόξως τοῦ θεοῦ τὰς τούτων ἁπάντων βουλὰς τῷ αὑτοῦ θεράποντι διὰ φασμάτων ἐκκαλύπτοντος. Eusebius, *Vita Constantini* I, 47. Cf. *Tricennal.* 18.

28. In general see H. Vörlander, *Mein Gott: Die Vorstellungen vom persönlichen Gott im Alten Orient und im Alten Testament* (Neukirchen-Vruyn, 1975); E. Peterson, "Der Gottesfreund," *Zeitschr. f. Kirchengesch.* 42 (1923), 161–198.

29. O. Neugebauer and H. B. van Hoesen, *Greek Horoscopes*, p. 126; see F. Millar, *The Emperor in the Roman World*, pp. 115–117, 465–477.

30. A. J. Festugière, "L'expérience religieuse du médecin Thessalos," *Revue Biblique* 48 (1939), 45–77 = *Hermétisme et mystique païenne* (Paris, 1967), pp. 141–180 at p. 151.

31. Festugière, *Hermétisme*, p. 162. Cf. Cyprian, *Ad. Fort.* 13, on Paul: *Dignatione divina ad tertium caelum adque in paradisum raptus . . . ad claritatem tantam pervenire, ut amicus Dei fiat.*

32. E. R. Dodds, *Pagan and Christian*, pp. 37–53; Martine Dulaey, *Le rêve dans la vie et la pensée de Saint Augustin* (Paris, 1973), esp. pp. 15–31.

33. Aelius Aristides, *Sacred Tales* IV, 52, Behr, p. 265.

34. *Passio Perpetuae* 4, 1, Musurillo, p. 110.

35. Artemidorus, *Oneirocriticon* II, 54, p. 183.22.

120   NOTES TO PAGES 66–69

36. Artemidorus, *Oneirocriticon* II, 52, p. 183.1.
37. Artemidorus, *Oneirocriticon* II, 53, p. 183.15.
38. Artemidorus, *Oneirocriticon* II, 53, p. 183.9.
39. Artemidorus, *Oneirocriticon* II, 51, p. 182.24.
40. *Mart. Polycarp.* 2, Musurillo pp. 4, 7–8.
41. *Passio Perpetuae* 1, 4, Musurillo, p. 106, citing *Acts* 2, 17–18, which cites *Joel* 2, 28; See T. D. Barnes, *Tertullian*, p. 77.
42. Irenaeus, *Adversus Haereses* V, 6, 1.
43. A. von Harnack, "Die Lehre der Zwölf Apostel," *Texte und Untersuchungen* 2.1 and 2.2 (Leipzig, 1884), p. 37.
44. Tertullian, *De anima* 9, 4: *Iamvero prout scripturae leguntur aut psalmi canuntur aut allocutiones proferuntur aut petitiones delegantur, ita inde materiae visionibus subministrantur.*
45. Hermas, *Pastor*, Mand. XI, 43, 6; see J. Reiling, *Hermas and Christian Prophecy: A Study of the Eleventh Mandate*, Suppl. to *Novum Testamentum* 37 (Leiden, 1973).
46. P. de Labriolle, *La crise montaniste* (Paris, 1913), p. 110: "Chose curieuse, jusque dans ses rigeurs même le Paraclet conservait une modération relative."
47. Tertullian, *De virg. vel.* 17, 3.
48. E. R. Dodds, *Pagan and Christian*, p. 29.
49. Plutarch, *De fac. lunae* 28, 943A: τὸν ἄνθρωπον οἱ πολλοὶ σύνθετον μὲν ὀρθῶς ἐκ δυεῖν δὲ, μόνον σύνθετον οὐκ ὀρθῶς ἡγοῦνται. μόριον γὰρ εἶναί πως ψυχῆς οἴονται τὸν νοῦν, οὐδὲν ἧττον ἐκείνων ἁμαρτάνοντες οἷς ἡ ψυχὴ δοκεῖ μόριον εἶναι τοῦ σώματος· νοῦς γὰρ ψυχῆς ὅσῳ σώματος ἄμεινον ἐστι καὶ θειότερον.
50. A. Henrichs and L. Koenen, "Der Kölner Mani-Kodex (P. Colon. inv. nr. 4780: Περὶ τῆς γέννης τοῦ σώματος αὐτοῦ)," *Zeitschr. f. Papyrologie und Epigraphik* 19 (1975), 24, 3 at p. 27.
51. *Pan. Lat.* 7.21, 4 ff.
52. S. G. MacCormack, "Roma, Constantinopolis, the Emperor and His Genius," *Classical Quarterly* 25 (1975), 131–150 at p. 131.
53. A. D. Nock, "The Emperor's Divine *Comes*," *Journal of Roman Studies* 37 (1947), 102–116 at p. 104 = *Essays*, pp. 653–675 at p. 656.
54. This is demonstrated by immunity from sorcery, due to the superior power of the protector: Plotinus–Porphyry, *Vita Plotini* 10; the Emperor Constantius–Ammianus Marcellinus, XIX, xii, 16 (see S. G. MacCormack, *Class. Quart.* 25 (1975), 137–138); Ambrose–Paulinus, *Vita Ambrosii* 20. It is the same in Jewish circles: H. L. Strack and P. Billerbeck, *Kommentar zum Neuen Testament aus Talmud and Midrasch* IV, 1 (Munich, 1961), 528, *Tanch. Mishpatim* 99a: "Da sieht man, wenn er reich ist an Gebotserfüllungen, so behü-

ten ihn zehntausend und tausend Engeln, und wenn er vollkommen ist an Torahkenntnis und guten Werken, so behütet ihn Gott."

55. Ammianus Marcellinus, XXI, 14, 3.

56. E. Peterson, "Der Gottesfreund," p. 193: "Was bei Clemens gewöhnlich ἀγάπη gemeint wird, heisst hier φιλία, und was bei Clemens auf Christus konzentriert erscheint, verteilt sich hier, auf einem Reich von δυνάμεις."

57. Origen, De oratione 31.

58. Origen, In Num. hom. 20, 3.

59. Origen, In Lev. hom. 11, 11.

60. Origen, Peri Archôn VII, 5.

61. Origen, De Susanna, P. G. 11.44A.

62. Gerald Manley Hopkins, The Wreck of the Deutschland (1876), chap. 10.

63. Augustine, Confessions, V, xiii, 23.

64. Grégoire le Thaumaturge, Remerciement à Origène, 43, 4, Sources chrétiennes 148, ed. H. Crouzel (Paris, 1969), p. 114. That the guardian angel was regarded as the principle of a person's identity is shown in Jerome's opening sentences to his description of the life of his heroine Paula in Ep. 108, 2: Testor Jesum et sanctos angelos eius ipsumque proprie angelum, qui custos fuit et comes admirabilis feminae. Eventually angelus is used as a courtesy phrase for the person. See Collectio Avellana, no. 187, line 3 (C.S.E.L. 35, 644.20): ut ad nos angelus vester destinare dignetur. See also W. E. Crum and H. G. Evelyn, The Monastery of Epiphanius (New York, 1926), vol. II, no. 113, and H. Grégoire, "'Ton ange' et les anges de Thera," Byzantinische Zeitschrift 30 (1929–30), 641–644. (I owe these references to the kindness of Leslie MacCoull.)

65. A. Henrichs and L. Koenen, "Ein griechischer Mani-Kodex," Zeitschr. f. Papyrologie u. Epigraphik 5 (1970), 139.

66. Henrichs and Koenen, "Kölner Mani-Kodex," Zeitschr. f. Papyrologie u. Epigraphik 19 (1975), 20.8 at p. 23. Mani, we may add, met his match in Kartīr. This leader of the Zoroastrian clergy saw his position as éminence grise of the Sasanian Empire in terms of a vision of his double–his daēna–and of the after-life: Philippe Gignoux, "L'inscription de Kartir à Sar Mašhad," Journal Asiatique 256 (1968), 387–418, lines 35–55, at pp. 401–405, and commentary at pp. 407–408 and no. 80, pp. 417–418; and in a more fragmentary manner at Naqš-i Rustam: C. J. Brunner, "The Middle Persian Inscription of the priest Kardēr at Naqš-i Rustam," Near Eastern Numismatics, Iconography, Epigraphy, and History: Studies in Honour of George C. Miles (American University of Beirut, 1974) at p. 97.

67. *Mart. Justini* 4, 7–8, Musurillo, p. 50.

68. Such strains, though felt, could be counteracted by the solidarity of the immigrant group and its ability to create a home away from home, e.g., *Bull. corr. hell. 9* (1885), 128.41: ἵνα ὥσπερ ἀποικία τις ᾖ δῆμος ἡμέτερος οὐ ξένος οὐδὲ ἀλλότριος ἀλλὰ ἐγχώριος παρὰ Ῥωμαίοις διατελῇ.

69. C. Andresen, *Logos und Nomos* (Berlin, 1955), esp. p. 114.

70. F. J. Dölger, *Der Exorzismus im altchristl. Taufritual* (Paderborn 1909).

71. Exorcism was invariably conceived of as the recreation of order in that part of the universe that had been disrupted by anomalous elements, e.g., Ps. Clement, *Recognitiones* I, 15–16: *mare statutum terminum servat, angeli pacem custodiunt, stellae ordinem tenent . . . daemones quoque certum est timore in fugam verti.*

72. H. L. Strack and P. Billerbeck, *Kommentar zum Neuen Testament* IV, 1, pp. 501–535 at p. 506.

73. The sexual element in this has been exaggerated by modern scholars. In the ancient world, lovemaking—and the good cheer that would go with it—was considered the occasion on which tongues were loosed and important secrets revealed. See Artemidorus, *Oneirocriticon* I, 78, p. 88.20 and I, 80, p. 97.9, and *Testament of the Twelve Patriarchs,* Judah 6, 4: "Moreover wine revealeth the mysteries of God and men, even the mysteries of Jacob my father to the Canaanitish woman Bathsheba, which God bade me not reveal." Cf. *Enoch,* esp. 16, 3: "And these in the hardness of their hearts you have made known to the women, and through these mysteries women and men work much evil on earth."

74. *Enoch* 8, 1.

75. *Enoch* 69, 6.

76. *Enoch* 69, 9.

77. *Enoch* 65, 6ff.: "Their ruin is accomplished because they have learnt all the secrets of the angels, and all the violence of the Satans, and all their powers—the most secret ones—and all the power of those who practise sorcery and the power of witchcraft, and the power of those who make molten images for the whole earth."

78. Tertullian, *De idololatria* IX, 1–2 *o divina sententia usque ad terram pertinax.*

79. The role of the guardian angel in Apuleius, *De deo Socratis* 16—*mala averruncare, bona prosperare, humilia sublimare, nutantia fulcire, obscura clarere*—is similar to the effects ascribed to baptism (which included the action of a purifying angel, Tertullian, *De baptismo* VI, 1: *sed in aqua emendati sub angelo*) by Cyprian, *Ad dom.* 4: *confirmari se*

dubia, patere clausa, lucere tenebrosa, facultatem dare quod prius difficile videbatur.

80. Marius Victorinus, *Ad Gal.* 2, 3, *P.L.* 8, 1175–1176.

81. R. Reitzenstein, *Poimandres* (Leipzig, 1904), p. 80.

82. Tatian, *Oratio c. Graecos* 9.

83. Firmicus Maternus, *Mathesis* II, 29, 10.

84. *Excerpta Theodoti* 69, *P.G.* 9, 692 AB: Ἡ εἱμαρμένη ἐστὶ σύνοδος πολλῶν καὶ ἐναντίων δυνάμεων.

85. *Excerpta Theodoti* 72, *P.G.* 9, 692C.

86. Origen, *Contra Celsum* VIII, 1. Christian attitudes needed so much explanation that one is tempted to think that *qui s'excuse s'accuse,* e.g., Ps.-Clement, II, 71, 1: *non pro superbia, O Clemens, convivium non ago cum his qui nondum purificati sunt,* and IV.33, *Numquid nos alterius sumus naturae superioris alicuius et propterea nos daemones timent? Unius eiusdemque vobiscum naturae sumus sed religione differimus, quod si et vos esse vultis non invidemus.* Whatever the origin of the *Recognitiones* in an exclusive group, it was accepted as part of the common Christian literature of its time.

87. For the rising costs of outlays in Asia Minor see W. Ruge, s.v. "Tekmoreioi," *Pauly Realencyclopädie* (Stuttgart, 1934), pp. 158–169 at p. 163; in Africa, R. Duncan-Jones, *The Economy of the Roman Empire* (Cambridge, 1974), p. 66; in Palestine, D. Sperber, *Roman Palestine 200–400: Money and Prices* (Ramat-Gan, 1974), p. 142: "In the past, when money was to be found, people were eager to listen to lessons in Mishna, Halacha and Talmud. But now that money is no longer to be found and they suffer so much from the affliction, they wish to hear only words of blessing and support."

88. Tertullian, *De anima* 57, 3.

89. *Passio Perpetuae* 7, 1–2, Musurillo, p. 114.

90. *Passio Perpetuae* 7, 6, Musurillo, p. 114. Cf. Apuleius, *Apologia* 43–44, on the stigma of epilepsy in a small town.

91. *Passio Perpetuae* 8, 4, Musurillo, p. 116. Cf. 12, 6, Musurillo, p. 120: *ite et ludite.* For Adam and Eve as playing children: R. Murray, *Symbols of Church and Kingdom* (Cambridge, 1975), pp. 304–306. For a slave to dream that he is a child is good, for he will be held blameless: Artemidorus, *Oneirocriticon* I, 13, p. 21.26.

92. *Passio Perpetuae* 5, 3, Musurillo, p. 112.

93. Minucius Felix, *Octavius* 38, 3 f.

94. H. Delehaye, *Sanctus* (Brussels, 1927), pp. 136–137.

95. W. M. Ramsay, *The Cities and Bishoprics of Asia Minor* (Oxford, 1897), pp. 484–568, esp. pp. 517 and 532.

96. Pontius, *Vita Cypriani* 5 and 6. For the constant presence of the

Christian crowd at the martyrdom: *Mart. Cypr.* 2, 5, Musurillo, p. 170, and 5, 1 and 6, Musurillo, p. 172; he had to control it: *Ep.* 5, 2: but it explains his choice as bishop: M. Sage, *Cyprian*, pp. 142–143.

97. Pontius, *Vita Cypriani* 7; see M. Sage, *Cyprian*, pp. 132–134.

98. Pontius, *Vita Cypriani* 3. For the fourth century, see E. Patlagean, "Sur la limitation de la fécondité dans la haute époque byzantine," *Annales* 24 (1969), 1353–1369 at p. 1366. It is good for a rich man to dream that he has a river running from his house: Artemidorus, *Oneirocriticon* II, 27, p. 49.2: πολλοί τε ἐπὶ τὴν οἰκίαν αὐτοῦ φοιτήσουσι δεόμενοι καὶ χρήξοντες.

99. Cyprian, *Ep.* 48, 4: *perficiet divina protectio, ut Dominus qui sacerdotes sibi in ecclesia sua eligere et constituere dignatur, electos quoque et constitutos sua voluntate atque opitulatione tueatur, gubernanter inspirans et subministrans.* See J. Speigl, "Cyprian über das *iudicium* bei der Bischofseinsetzung," *Röm. Quartalschrift* 69 (1974), 30–45. This aspect of Cyprian is fully described by A. V. Harnack, "Cyprian als Enthusiast," *Zeitschr. f. neutestam. Wiss.* 3 (1902), 177–191; but Harnack's rigid periodization of Christian history into a "charismatic" and a "post-charismatic" phase makes Cyprian a puzzling figure to him. Harnack's difficulty springs from misunderstanding the nature and overall prevalence of belief in inspiration and protection in the third century.

100. Cyprian, *Ep.* 40, 1: *admonitos nos et instructos sciatis dignatione divina.*

101. *Mart. Cypr.* 4, 1, Musurillo p. 172. It was vital that he should be executed at Carthage: *Ep.* 81, 1: *caeterum mutilabitur honor ecclesiae nostrae tam gloriosae.*

102. Cyprian, *Ep.* 38, 1: *quem sic Dominus honoravit caelistis gloriae dignitate.* Cf. S. Mazzarino, *Antico, tardoantico*, p. 175.

103. Cyprian, *Ep.* 31, 2, letter of the *confessores: ex tuis ergo litteris videmus gloriosos illos martyrum triumphos.* The art of the Late Roman panegyrist consisted of conjuring up just such visual images: S. G. MacCormack, *Rev. études augustiniennes* 22 (1976), 46–54.

104. Vivid images of public munificence: Cyprian, *De op. elymos.* 21/22: *si in gentilium munere grande et gloriosum videtur proconsules vel imperatores habere praesentes; Ep,* 37, 2: the imagery of the seasons connected with the annual consular *dignitas* enjoyed by the martyrs.

105. Cyprian, *Ep.* 66, 10.

106. Inscription of Cyril Celer at Laodicaea Combusta: *Monumenta Asiae Minoris Antiqua* I (London, 1928), no. 170, p. 89: βουλήσει τοῦ παντοκράτορος θεοῦ ἐπίσκοπος κατασταθ[εί]ς.

107. Aquileia: G. Cuscito, "Gradi e funzioni ecclesiastiche negli

epigrafi dell' alto adriatico orientale," *Antichità Altoadriatiche* 6 (Trieste, 1974), 211–244 at p. 211: *poemnio caelitus tibi traditum*. This is well seen by S. Mazzarino, "Costantino e l'episcopato," *Iura* 7 (1956), 345–353, in *Antico, tardoantico*, pp. 171–182.

108. This would explain the local witticism at the expense of the great Donatist bishop of the late fourth century, Optatus of Timgad: *quod comitem haberet deum* "The Count (of Africa, Gildo) is his God"— Augustine, *Contra litteras Petiliani* II, xxii, 53. The bishop must have been thought to have God himself as his divine *comes*.

4 FROM THE HEAVENS TO THE DESERT

1. *Apophthegmata Patrum*, Poimen 183, *P.G.* 65, 365D.

2. For a firm and judicious rebuttal of this view, see H. Torp, "The Carved Decorations of the North and South Churches at Bawit," *Kolloquium über spätantiken und frühmittelalterlichen Skulptur*, ed. V. Miločić (Mainz, 1970), p. 41. "To be sure, attempts have been made to elevate to the rank of principles of art history sharply drawn, ethnic religious distinctions between Copts, Greeks, and Latins. But this has not been without disastrous effects on the study of Coptic art history. It is well to remember that at Sohag, both in the Red Monastery from about A.D. 500 and in the contemporary White Monastery of Shenūti, the Greco-Roman language rises to a magnificent climax just in the trefoil chancel, the architectural and spiritual center of the buildings. Undoubtedly, the 'Roman' chancel of the great patriot Shenūti teaches that the alleged contrast between Mediterranean art forms and the anti-Roman and anti-Byzantine sentiment of the Copts, cannot but be the fruit of modern art historical speculation. Seven or eight centuries after Alexander's conquest, the vocabulary of classical architecture with its rich plastic articulation surely was felt by the Copts to be part of the legacy of the land, a legacy sanctified by its association with the great sanctuaries of the new creed, in the Holy Land, in Alexandria and along the Nile."

3. This has been translated by Benedicta Ward, *The Sayings of the Desert Fathers* (Oxford, 1975).

4. *Apophthegm*. Macarius 2, 260D.

5. *Apophthegm*. Poimen 110, 349BC.

6. A. Cohen, *Arab Border-Village in Israel* (Manchester, 1965), p. 59.

7. E.g., H. I. Bell, V. Martin, E. G. Turner, and D. van Berchem, *The Abinnaeus Archive* (Oxford, 1962), for a vivid glimpse into the tensions of mid-fourth century villages: esp. no. 28, p. 77, and no. 57,

p. 108. On the ancient Egyptian peasant as he emerges in Chester Beatty, *Pap.* III, a dreambook of 2000–1755 B.C.: S. Sauneron, *Les songes et leur interprétation*, Sources Orientales 2 (Paris, 1959), p. 38: "batailleur, beau parleur, et acharné à défendre les pauvres biens qu'un sort misérable lui a laissé."

8. *Apophthegm.* Matoes 13, 293C.

9. A. H. M. Jones, *The Later Roman Empire*, II, 780.

10. A. C. Johnson and L. C. West, *Byzantine Egypt* (Princeton, 1949), p. 40.

11. Athanasius, *V. Antonii*, 2, trans. R. T. Meyer, Ancient Christian Writers 10, C.U.A. (London, 1950), p. 20.

12. *Pachomii Vita Tertia* 45, ed. F. Halkin, *Sancti Pachomii Vitae Graecae* (Brussels, 1932), p. 280.

13. H. Braunert, *Die Binnenwanderung* (Bonn, 1964), p. 266.

14. μηδεμίαν τε συμπλοκὴν⟨ν⟩ ἔχων πρὸς τινας κατὰ τὴν κώμην ἀλλὰ κατὰ ἐμαυτὸν ἀναχωροῦντος. A. E. Boak and H. C. Youtie, *The Archive of Aurelius Isidore* (Ann Arbor, 1960), no. 75, pp. 295–296.

15. Athanasius, *Vita Antonii* 2, Meyer p. 19.

16. Philip Larkin, "Poetry of Departures," *The Less Deceived* (Hull, 1955), p. 34.

17. *Apophthegm.* Agatho 10, 112 C: ἄοκνος ἐν τῷ σωματικῷ καὶ αὐτάρκης ἐν πᾶσιν. It is important to remember the comparatively wide area of economic activity open in Egypt to the independent man as an artisan and seasonal laborer. See esp. I. F. Fichmann, *Egipet na rubezhe dvukh epokh* (Moscow, 1965), p. 210.

18. Françoise-E. Morard, *Monachos, moine, histoire du terme grec jusqu'au 4ème siècle* (Fribourg en Suisse, 1973), from *Freiburger Zeitschr. f. Philosophie und Theologie* 20 (1973), 332–425, at pp. 362–378.

19. This aspect has been unduly stressed in explaining asceticism by scholars who rely on one deeply Hellenized source, the *Lausiac History* of Palladius. See, e.g., E. R. Dodds, *Pagan and Christian*, pp. 29–36.

20. Palladius, *Historia Lausiaca* 23.

21. Artemidorus, *Oneirocriticon* I, 78, p. 86.23.

22. *Apophthegm.* Olympios 2, 313D–316A.

23. *Apophthegm.* Isidore 2, 220C.

24. *Apophthegm.* Isidore 5, 221B.

25. *Apophthegm.* Agatho 15, 113B.

26. *Apophthegm.* Achillas 4, 125A.

27. *Apophthegm.* Macarius 23, 272C and Moses 11, 285D.

28. Serge Sauneron, "Fouilles d'Esna," *Bulletin de l'Institut d'Archéologie Orientale* 67 (1969), 100.

29. Palladius, *Historia Lausiaca* 22, 9.

30. As was R. W. Medlitcott, "St. Antony Abbot and the Hazards of Asceticism," *British Journal of Medical Psychology* 42 (1969), 133–140.

31. See above p. 68.

32. Athanasius, *Vita Antonii* 10, Meyer, p. 29: "I will ever be your helper and I will make you renowned everywhere."

33. Every monk had his βοηθός: P. Nau, "Histoires des solitaires d'Egypte," *Revue de l'Orient Chrétien* 13.190 (1908), 274–275.

34. Athanasius, *Vita Antonii* 14, Meyer, p. 32.

35. A. D. Nock, "Hellenistic Mysteries and Christian Sacrements," *Mnemosyne*, ser. 4.5 (1952), p. 191 = *Essays*, 802.

36. See above p. 74, n. 71.

37. *Apophthegm.* Poimen 67, 337C: τὰ γὰρ θελήματα ἡμῶν δαίμονες γεγόνασι καὶ αὐτοί εἰσιν οἱ θλίβοντες ἡμᾶς, ἵνα πληρώσωμεν αὐτά. Ps.-Clement, *Recognitiones* II, 72, 1: *ut ipsorum ministerio cupiditates eorum expleant.* Cf. *Recogn.* IV, 16, and Ps.-Clement, *Hom.* IX, 9, 2.

38. *Apophthegm.* Pityrio, 376A: οἵου γὰρ ἂν πάθους περιγένηταί τις τούτου καὶ τὸν δαίμονα ἀπελαύνει.

39. *Apophthegm.* Poimen 32, 329D.

40. Esaias, *Asceticon* XV, 76, C.S.C.O. 294, p. 300.

41. *Apophthegm.* Macarius 39, 380C; Olympios 1, 313 CD.

42. Athanasius, *Vita Antonii* 72, Meyer, p. 80, *Pachomii Vita Prima* 82, Halkin, p. 55.

43. *Apophthegm.* Anub 1, 129 A.

44. For the hardening of attitudes, see Martine Dulaey, *Le rêve*, p. 52.

45. Eusebius, *Hist. Eccles.* VI, 41, 2.

46. A. J. Festugière, *La révélation d'Hermès Trismégiste* I (Paris, 1950), 313; see C. H. Roberts, *Museum Helveticum* 10 (1952), 272, and *Pap. Oxy.* 2332.

47. R. Rémondon, "L'Egypte et la suprême résistance au christianisme," *Bull. Instit. Franç. d'Archéologie Orientale* 51:(1952), 63–78; H. Torp, "Leda Christiana: The Problem of the Interpretation of Coptic Sculpture with Mythological Motifs," *Acta Instit. Rom. Norvegiae* 4 (1969), 101–112.

48. Eusebius, *Demonstratio Evangelica* VIII, 1.

49. P. Nau, "Histoires." *Rev. de l'Orient Chrét.* 13.191 (1908), 275.

50. *Apophthegm.* Ammoe 4, 128 A.

51. *Apophthegm.* Matoes 2, 289C.

52. F. Nau, "Histoires." *Rev. de l'Orient Chrét.* 17.332 (1912), 210.

53. *Apophthegm.* Olympios 1, 313CD.

54. *Apophthegm.* Anthony 30, 85B.

55. Lay people needed visions: H. I. Bell, *Jews and Christian in Egypt* (London, 1924), pp. 108–109—a woman writing to the hermit Paphnutios: B.M. Pap. 1926, 8: οὕτως π⟨ι⟩στεύω διὰ τῶν σῶν εὐχῶν εἴασιν λαμβάνω. τῶν γὰρ ἀσκούντων καὶ θρησευόντων ἀποκλύνματα δικνέοντε.

56. *Apophthegm.* Arsenius 5 (49), 89A: ἀπὸ τῶν ἰδίων πόνων ἐκτήσαντο τὰς ἀρετάς.

57. On the vital importance of mourning and acute depressive states, see e.g., *Apophthegm.* Poimen 72, 340B and 144, 357D.

58. Robert Graves, *Collected Poems 1965* (London, 1965), p. 21.

59. J. H. Waszink, *Tertullian, De Anima* (Amsterdam, 1948), p. 169, for evidence of the considerable role of the καρδιογνώστης in Early Christian communities.

60. *Mart. Montani et Lucii* 11, Musurillo, p. 222. By contrast, the experience of transparency was not a dream welcomed by the readers of Artemidorus, who regularly dreaded the uncovering of hidden things: *Oneirocriticon* I, 44, p. 50.15; I, 66, p. 72.21; I, 67, p. 73.10.

61. Cyprian, *Testimonia* III, 56, I Sam. 16:7; also citing *Sap. Salom.* 15, 3: *In omni loco speculantur oculi Dei bonos et malos* and *Apocal.* 2, 23: *Et sciant omnes ecclesiae quia ego sum scrutator renis et cordis.*

62. Constantine, *"Aeterna et religiosa"*, August 314: *P.L.* 8.487C. Cf. Cyprian, *Ad. Don.* 9: *o si et possis in illa sublimi specula constitutus oculos tuos inserere secretis.*

63. Cyprian, *De lapsis* 25: *tanta est potestas Domini, tanta maiestas: secreta tenebrarum sub eius luce detecta sunt, sacerdotem Dei nec occulta crimina fefellerunt.*

64. Constantine, "κακὸς ἑρμηνεὺς," *P.L.* 8. 518C.

65. *Pachomii vita prima* 112, Halkin, p. 73.

66. *Pachomii regula* 77 (lxvii), ed. A. Boon and L. Th. Lefort, *Pachomiana latina* (Louvain, 1932), p. 35.

67. *Epistula Ammonis* 21, Halkin, p. 110.

68. *Apophthegm.* Marcarius 32, 273D; *Const. Apost.* XI, 26. See the admirable study of Philip Rousseau, "The Spiritual Authority of the 'Monk-bishop': Eastern Elements in Some Western Hagiography of the Fourth and Fifth Centuries," *Journal of Theological Studies* n.s. 22 (1971), 380–419.

69. For the Pope as *deus terrenus* in later medieval thought: M. Maccarone, *Vicarius Christi* (Rome, 1952), pp. 237–238 and 254.

70. *Sancti Pachomii vita quarta* 1, Halkin, p. 407.

71. *Apophthegm.* Poimen 125. 353C; H. Döries, "Die Beicht im alten Mönchtum," *Festchr. f. Joachim Jeremias, Beiträge z. Zeitschr. f. neutestam. Wiss.* 26 (Berlin, 1960), 234–242 at 236: "An der Würzel des Mönchtums steht ein vertieftes Sündenbewusstsein."

72. Themistius, *Oratio* XIII, 178A, on the Senate of Rome: δι' ὑμᾶς τοι, ὦ μακάριοι, οἱ θεοὶ τὴν γῆν οὔπω ἀπολελοίπασι, καὶ ὑμεῖς ἐστὲ οἱ μέχριτέως ἀπομαχόμενοι μὴ παντάπασι τὴν θνητὴν φύσιν τῆς ἀθανάτου ἀπορραγῆναι.

73. Ammianus Marcellinus, XXI, 1.8.

74. Richard Gordon, "The Sacred Geography of a *Mithraeum:* The Example of Sette Sfere," *Journal of Mithraic Studies* 1 (1976), 145.

75. Plotinus, *Enneads* II, 9, 9, trans. Stephen MacKenna (London 1962), p. 141; on this see C. Elsas, *Neuplatonische und gnostische Weltablehnung in der Schule Plotins* (Berlin, 1976).

76. Paulinus, *Carmen* XIX, 18: *sic sacra disposuit terris monumenta piorum, / sparsit ut astrorum nocturno lumina caelo.*

77. Rabbinic Judaism reflects a similar development, P. Schäfer, *Rivalität zwischen Engeln und Menschen*, Studia Judaica (Berlin, 1975), esp. p. 233: "Der Mensch richtet sich nicht mehr nach der von der Engeln garantierten Harmonie des Cosmos, sondern die himmlische Ordnung ist von der irdischen Ordnung abhängig." On the contrast of Pelagius and Augustine, see G. Greshake, *Gnade als konkrete Freiheit* (Mainz, 1972), pp. 248–252, esp. p. 250: "Nicht mehr das Heilsgeschichtlich—'Kosmologische,' sondern das Personal-Subjektive nimmt den ersten Rang ein." On the failure to maintain a purely cosmic imagery in art from the early fourth century onwards see G. M. A. Hanfmann, *The Season Sarcophagus in Dumbarton Oaks*, I, 203 and 224.

78. Iamblichus, *De mysteriis* I, 8 (28.6), ed. E. des Places (Paris, 1966), p. 55.

INDEX